JEPHTHAH AND HIS VOW

JEPHTHAH AND HIS VOW

David Marcus

Texas Tech Press
Lubbock, Texas, U.S.A.
1986

ISBN 0-89672-135-3 (paper)
ISBN 0-89672-136-1 (cloth)
Library of Congress Catalog Card Number: 85-51356
Texas Tech Press
Texas Tech University
Lubbock, Texas 79409

Printed in the United States of America

CONTENTS

INTRODUCTION

Popularity of the Theme

The story of Jephthah and his vow has not only attracted the attention of many generations of Bible scholars but has also gripped the imagination of creative artists from ancient to modern times. It has served as an inspiration for the composition of dramas, poems, novels, songs, cantatas, oratorios, and operas. So popular has the story been that in 1948 W. O. Sypherd, a professor of English, was able to compile material sufficient for an entire book documenting where the theme has been used in literature, music, painting, and the allied arts (engraving, sculpture, manuscript illustration, and tapestry).[1] It is incredible how widespread are the various treatments of the story. Sypherd documented over 300 literary works in nearly every modern language, ranging in time from the middle ages till the late 1940s. In the musical sphere, where the oratorio has been the most popular medium of expressing the theme, Sypherd listed more than 100 oratorios, including the well-known *Jephte* by George Frederick Handel.[2]

The reason why the story of Jephthah and his daughter has appealed so widely to the creative imagination is because of the "impressive emotional qualities and dramatic possibilities which it presents or suggests."[3] While some of these works introduce modifications to the biblical text as, for example, divine intervention,[4] most are based on the traditional interpretation of the story in chapter 11 of the Book of Judges. Jephthah, newly elected as leader over Israel, is about to engage the Ammonites in war. Directly before the battle he makes a vow that should the Lord grant him victory he will sacrifice to Him the first person who greets him from his house on his successful return from battle. To Jephthah's profound dismay, his only daughter is the first to greet him and, after a two-month respite, he sacrifices her.

While this traditional interpretation, with its literal sacrifice of the daughter, has formed the basis for most of the artistic works mentioned,[5] some artists have interpreted the ending in a different manner. In their view the daughter was sacrificed only in a metaphorical sense: she was not put to death but had to remain as a virgin, consecrated to God, for the rest of her life.[6]

It will be seen that these two interpretations found in the artistic world for the conclusion of the Jephthah story are also reflected in the more prosaic, if perhaps more erudite, pages of biblical scholarship. Likewise, it will be seen that as popular as the Jephthah story was in the artistic world, it was equally popular with biblical commentators. The fact that Jephthah could vow his daughter to death evoked a plethora of theological and philosophical dissertations.

Dissertations on the subject were prominent especially in the 17th and 18th centuries when efforts were made to rationalize and explain Jephthah's actions.[7] In the 19th century two monograph-length articles surveyed and analyzed most previous work on the topic,[8] and in our own century hardly a decade goes by without another article appearing on the subject.[9]

HISTORY OF THE EXEGESIS

The earliest Jewish interpretation found in Pseudo-Philo,[10] Josephus,[11] the Midrash,[12] and the Targum[13] was that the vow was literally carried out. For example, the Targum rendered Judges 11:39 as follows:

> At the end of two months she returned to her father. He did to her according to his vow, and she had not known a man. It was hence prohibited in Israel for anyone to offer up a son or daughter as a burnt offering as Jephthah, the Gileadite, had done. . . .[14]

This literal interpretation was the opinion too of the early Church fathers, who also wrestled with the theological implications of the sacrifice. Two examples of many must suffice here.[15] Origen compared the sacrifice of Jephthah's daughter with the death of the Christian martyrs:

> It is a matter of higher speculation to consider even slightly the rationale of those sacrifices which cleanse those for whom they are offered. Jephthah's sacrifice of his daughter should receive attention; it was by vowing it that he conquered the children of Ammon, and the victim approved his vow. . . .[16]

Chrysostom discerned in Jephthah's sacrifice an example of God's "providence and clemency": by permitting this sacrifice He prevented future sacrifices of this type.

> This sacrifice was a striking example of providence and clemency; and that it was in care for our race that He did not prevent that sacrifice. For if after that vow and promise He had forbidden the sacrifice, many also who were subsequent to Jephthah, in the expectation that God would not receive their vows, would have increased the number of such vows, and proceeding on their way would have fallen into child-murder. But now, by suffering this vow to be actually fulfilled, He put a stop to all such cases in the future.[17]

This view of literal sacrifice continued throughout the Middle Ages and is to be found in the commentaries of the Jewish exegetes Rashi (1040-1105) and Naḥmanides (1194-1270), the latter commenting that "the subject is to be understood in its plain meaning (*kipešûṭô*)."[18]

The first hint of a different opinion comes in the commentary of another medieval Jewish exegete, David Kimḥi (1160-1235). Adopting his father's novel interpretation of the apodosis of the vow,[19] he suggests a conclusion for the story to be that of a life of virginity, not literal sacrifice. In arguing against the literal view he points to the daughter's statement in verse 37:

> It is quite clear that he did not kill her because the text [in verse 37] does not say "I will mourn for my life", [but only "I will mourn for my virginity"]. This indicates that he did not kill her but rather that she did not know a man [remained a virgin], because the text says [verse 39] "she did not know a man."[20]

Another argument Kimḥi brings is the fact that the text does not actually state that Jephthah put his daughter to death: "Furthermore, the text in verse 39 goes on to say 'he fulfilled with her the vow which he had made.' It does not say 'he offered her up as an *'ôlāh*!"[21] In Kimḥi's view the daughter became a recluse (*perûšāh*): "He built her a house and placed her there. She became a recluse (*perûšāh*) from mankind and from the ways of the world."[22] Kimḥi's interpretation was adopted by other medieval Jewish exegetes such as Ralbag (Levi ben Gershon, 1288-1344)[23] and Abravanel (1437-1508),[24] and it can be found in the popular 18th century commentary of Yeḥiel Hillel Altschuler (Meṣudat David), which is printed in many Rabbinic Bibles. A number of Christian exegetes also adopted this non-literal conclusion approach, but under the influence of the medieval practice of nunnery they extended the interpretation of the ending of the story to include consecration at a sanctuary.[25]

In the 19th century the non-literal conclusion continued to be popular with some Jewish interpreters, such as the Malbim (Meir Loeb ben Yeḥiel Michael, 1809-1879),[26] and it also gained the adherence of critical scholars such as P. Cassel,[27] C. F. Keil and F. Delitzsch,[28] A. Köhler,[29] E. König,[30] and others.[31] However, most of their contemporaries, such as E. Bertheau,[32] J. S. Black,[33] K. Budde,[34] F. Buhl,[35] H. Ewald,[36] E. Renan,[37] G. L. Studer,[38] and J. Wellhausen,[39] favored the literal and sacrificial conclusion. The non-literal conclusion was generally denounced. For example, Ewald stated: "The timid modern notion, repeated even in the most recent books . . . that Jephthah did not really sacrifice his daughter, requires no further refutation."[40] Budde had only one word for the other theory: "nonsense" (*Unsinn*).[41]

In this century, apart from a few voices of dissension like those of I. Benzinger,[42] G. Boström,[43] M. Weinfeld,[44] and L. Wood,[45] there has been almost unanimous worldwide agreement for the literal conclusion. This can be seen in the commentaries of C. F. Burney, G. A. Cooke, Y. Kaufmann, G. F. Moore, F. Nötscher, V. Zapletal, and others on the Book of Judges.[46] This applies likewise to all the latest commentaries on the book in the last two decades, the four most recent being that of J. D. Martin in the Cambridge Bible Commentary on the New English Bible (1975), of R. G. Boling in The Anchor Bible series (1975), of J. Eliṣur (in Hebrew, 1976), and of J. A. Soggin in the Old Testament Library (1981). Similarly, this unanimity extends also to translators of the Bible, for by translating one of the verses in a certain fashion (as will be shown below)[47] a literal conclusion is obviously meant. The latest translation of which we are aware is the 1978 publication of *The Prophets* by the Jewish Publication Society, and this translation, too, suggests the literal conclusion. Outside of commentaries and translations, this view is held by most scholars writing histories, encyclopaedias, introductions, and studies touching on various details (e.g., human sacrifice) in the story.[48]

A Dissenting View

From the point of view of endorsement and sheer numbers, it would seem that the matter is beyond doubt, and that Luther's oft-repeated[49] marginal note "some affirm that he did not sacrifice her, but the text is clear enough"[50] is still as valid as ever. However, I believe that the case of the majority—hereafter, the sacrificialists—is not as ironclad as is often thought,[51] and that the minority opinion—hereafter, the non-sacrificialists—is not without merit. My position is based on two major points.

In the first place, it is rather simplistic and, in fact, wrong to believe that the text is "clear enough." As will be demonstrated in this study, the text of Judges 11:29-40 poses a number of textual questions, some of which are decidedly unclear. These questions are of various difficulty and affect those parts of the story dealing with the form of the vow, the status of the daughter, the daughter's requests, the fulfillment of the vow, and the aftermath.

As an illustration of these difficulties, we may look at the form of the vow in verse 31 where the Hebrew text reads:

wehāyāh hayyôṣē' 'ašer yēṣē' middaltê bêtî liqrā'tî bešûbî bešālôm mibbenê 'ammôn wehāyāh laYHWH weha'alîtīhû 'ôlāh	Whoever goes out from the doors of my house to greet me, when I return safely from the Ammonites, will belong to the Lord, and I will offer him up as an *'ôlāh*.[52]

At least three grammatical questions arise from this verse: (1) Why is there a double introductory formula, *hayyôṣē'* "whoever goes out" and *'ašer yēṣē'* "whoever goes out," when one would suffice? (2) Why is there an extra *wehāyāh* "and he will be" in the apodosis [= the promise]: *wehāyāh hayyôṣē'* "it will be that whoever goes out" and *wehāyāh laYHWH* "he will be [= belong] to the Lord"? Is this second *wehāyāh* "it / he will be" syntactically necessary or not? (3) Is there a textual dislocation here inasmuch as the regular idiom "to offer up an *'ôlāh* to the Lord" is *leha'alôt 'ôlāh laYHWH*? Did the phrase *laYHWH* originally belong with *'ôlāh* not with *wehāyāh* of the previous phrase? These questions are discussed in detail in chapter 1 when the form of the vow is analyzed.

Secondly, not all the arguments made by the non-sacrificialists can be lightly dismissed. The complexity of the problem may be illustrated by listing a number of the arguments both sides raise in connection with the wording of the vow and its fulfillment.

As regards the vow, the sacrificialists maintain that the phrase "I will offer him up as an *'ôlāh*" means unequivocally that Jephthah intended an actual sacrifice. A typical translation of the vow is that of Boling:[53]

> Jephthah made a vow to Yahweh; he said, "If you will really subject the Ammonites to my power, then anything coming out the doors of my house to meet me, when I return with victory from the Ammonites, shall belong to Yahweh; I will offer it up as a burnt offering."

The phrase *weha'alîtīhû 'ôlāh* is thought to mean exactly what it says, "I will offer it up as a burnt offering," and cannot denote consecration. Likewise with the completion of the vow in verse 39, again citing Boling's translation: "At the end of two months she returned to her father, and he fulfilled with her the vow which he had made."[54] The fulfillment which Jephthah effected was that of the second part of the vow made in verse 31: "I will offer it up as a burnt offering"; hence Jephthah's daughter was indeed sacrificed as a burnt offering.

On the other hand, the non-sacrificialists point out that the text does not state that Jephthah put his daughter to death. It does not say "he offered her up," but "he did to her as he had vowed." The fulfillment refers back to the first part of the vow in verse 31, namely, "he will belong to the Lord," and this phrase, as is the norm elsewhere, only means consecration. Hence the fulfillment of the vow was one of consecration, not of literal sacrifice. Support for this is to be found in the statement immediately following Jephthah's action: *wehî' lō' yāde'āh 'îš* "she did not know a man." Thus the daughter's remaining a consecrated virgin was the real result of Jephthah's vow.

THE CENTRAL QUESTION

The central question is this: are the arguments of the sacrificialists so overwhelming as to justify the almost unanimous one-sided support this conclusion has received in recent years? I believe that they are not and shall endeavor to demonstrate that in the course of this study.[55]

Since a large number of the arguments of both sides is based on the text, it is obvious that a correct interpretation of the story can only be accomplished when the textual questions, referred to above, are resolved. With some of these problems it will be shown that no resolution is possible, so that the text in some cases is simply ambiguous and open to different interpretations. But this very ambiguity should be enough to serve as a check on the undisputed interpretation of the majority side. If anything is "clear enough" it is that, from the text as it now stands, the fate of Jephthah's daughter cannot be determined with any finality.[56]

My method of procedure is to analyze the principal textual and exegetical questions arising from the story of Jephthah and his vow in the order in which they occur in the text. Chapter 1 deals with the wording of the vow described in verse 31 and considers (a) the question of whether Jephthah originally intended to sacrifice a human or an animal; (b) the form of the vow, its structure as compared to other vows in the Hebrew Bible, and the problems connected with the vow's apodosis; (c) whether the phrase "I will offer him/it up as an *'ôlāh*" has to be taken in its literal sense. Chapter 2 deals with the daughter's involvement in the story arising from verses 34-38 under the following headings: (a) whether the daughter is really Jephthah's only child; (b) why Jephthah mourned upon seeing her emerge from the house; (c) what the meaning is of the daughter's requests: to go "down" on the mountains and to lament her virginity for two months. Chapter 3 considers the fulfillment and aftermath of the vow as described in verse 39-40. The three principal questions in this chapter are: (a) is the phrase "she did not know a man" to be taken as circumstantial (which would then simply describe the condition of Jephthah's daughter at the time of her death, that is, she died a virgin) or consequential (which would reflect what actually happened to the daughter, that is, she lived a life of virginity)? (b) to whom or what does the phrase "to become a custom" refer? (c) what is the nature of the annual festival? is it one of mourning or commemoration? Chapter 4 deals with external considerations which have often been raised as having bearing on the story of Jephthah and his vow. First, the parallels with the Isaac story in Genesis 22 are considered; then the motifs in our story which occur in classical and other literatures are examined. Finally, an analysis is made of the likelihood in ancient Israel of a woman's electing to remain celibate, or alternatively, that Jephthah's vow represents an example of a human sacrifice offered in emergency conditions. Chapter 5 presents a summary of all the arguments, and the thesis is posited that since a number of the problems can have no resolution because they are ambivalent, it is this very ambivalence which was what the narrator or later editor had in mind.[57] I shall show that the narrator was an excellent craftsman and stylist, so that those parts of the story which are ambiguous could well have been deliberate on his part. The reader or listener is not meant to know, nor was it thought necessary for him to know, precisely how the action is resolved. In this way the tension is maintained and the suspense increased.

Because of this deliberate equivocation on the part of the narrator, I further suggest that the fate of Jephthah's daughter may not have been the chief element in the story at all, but rather Jephthah's rash vow. This suggestion is supported by two facts. First, Jewish tradition mostly referred to the Jephthah story, not so much because of the death of his daughter, nor because of the annual festival, but precisely because of the rashness of Jephthah's vow. Secondly, when one considers that the motif of an individual's not being careful with his speech occurs a number of times in the Book of Judges (as well as in the rest of the Hebrew Bible), it is quite possible that this may have been the main motif in the Jephthah story as well.

The first examples of the narrator's deliberate equivocations are to be found in the verse describing Jephthah's vow. It is this verse, with its several problems of exegesis and grammar, which is the subject of Chapter 1.

THE VOW: VERSE 31

Jephthah's vow occurs in Judges 11:31 and reads as follows:

wehāyāh hayyôṣē' 'ašer yēṣē' middaltê bêtî liqrā'tî bešûbî bešālôm mibbenê 'ammôn wehāyāh laYHWH weha'alîtīhû 'ôlāh	Whoever goes out from the doors of my house to greet me, when I return safely from the Ammonites, will belong to the Lord, and I will offer him up as an *'ôlāh*.

Several exegetical and grammatical questions arise from this verse: (1) What was the original intention of Jephthah when he made the vow: did he mean to vow an animal or a human being? (2) How does the structure of this vow compare with other vows found elsewhere in the Hebrew Bible? (3) How are the grammatical questions, alluded to above, to be explained? Namely, (a) why is there a double introductory formula, *hayyôṣē'* "whoever goes out" and *'ašer yēṣē'* "whoever goes out," when one would suffice? (b) why is there an extra *wehāyāh* in the apodosis, *wehāyāh hayyôṣē' . . . wehāyāh laYHWH*? Is this second *wehāyāh* syntactically necessary or not? (c) is there a textual dislocation here since the regular idiom "to offer up an *'ôlāh* to the Lord" is *leha'alôt 'ôlāh laYHWH*? Did the phrase *laYHWH* originally belong with *'ôlāh* and not with *wehāyāh* of the previous phrase? (4) does the phrase "I will offer him up as an *'ôlāh*" have to mean literal sacrifice? Each of the above questions will be discussed in order.

Original Intent of the Vow

The first question, which has been, and still is, strongly debated by biblical scholars, is what Jephthah's original intention was when he made the vow: did he mean to offer an animal or a human being? I believe that, from the text as it now stands, and in the light of other arguments, the weight of evidence seems to be that Jephthah intended an individual, not an animal. This conclusion is based on the language of the vow, the testimony of the ancient versions, and auxiliary arguments.

The Language of the Vow

The language of the vow appears to be inappropriate for animals. Three of the phrases in the apodosis [= the promise] of the vow are not found elsewhere with animals. The first phrase:

wehāyāh hayyôṣē' 'ašer yēṣē' . . . liqrā'tî	Whoever goes out . . . to greet me

Here two locutions with identical meanings (*hayyôṣē'* and *'ašer yēṣē'*) are used where one would have been sufficient (see further, p. 22). Neither of these expressions is used with animals, but both are used with people.[1] In addition, the occurrence of the verb *yāṣā'* with the verbal form *liqrā't* forms an idiom meaning "to go out to meet or greet someone," and it, too, is only found with people.[2] Indeed, Jephthah's daughter fulfills the conditions of the vow by coming out (*yṣ'*) to greet (*liqrā't*) her father (verse 34). Likewise, the women in the time of Saul and David came out (*yṣ'*) to greet (*liqrā't*) King Saul (1 Samuel, 18:6) upon his return from battle.

It is true that *liqrā't* is found once with an animal in Judges 14:5, *wehinnēh kefîr 'arāyôt šō'ēg liqrā'tô* "Suddenly a full-grown lion came roaring to meet him,"[3] but there is no verb *yāṣā'* here, nor is the phrase *yāṣā' liqrā't* said of an animal.

The second phrase:

wehāyāh hayyôṣē' 'ašer yēṣē' middaltê bêtî liqrā'tî	Whoever goes out from the doors of my house to greet me

The vowed item is said to come out of the doors of Jephthah's house. There is no reason why this literal interpretation cannot stand (see further, p. 16). In Joshua 2:19, which is its only other occurrence, the same phrase is used to connote the inside of a house as contrasted with the outside: "If anyone ventures outside the doors of your house (*daltê bêtēk*)." The question which has to be asked then is: is it likely that animals and people lived in the same house, so that an animal could possibly come out of the "doors of the house"? Lately, Boling has argued in favor of this suggestion, and in his *Commentary* has offered a reconstruction and a plan of a typical Iron Age house which shows that there were accommodations for the livestock as well as for the family in such a house:

> Because there were rooms built on three sides of a court, there was plenty of space to house such animals as sheep, cows, goats. It was reasonable, therefore, for Jephthah to assume that the first creature to wander out of his house when he returned would be an animal acceptable for sacrifice, and not his daughter.[4]

However, even if it can be demonstrated that men and animals lived under the same roof, it seems more likely that the phrase *daltê bêtî* refers to people rather than animals because the only other occurrence of the phrase refers to people, and it is used here together with *yāṣā' liqrā't*, which is only used with people.[5]

The third phrase:

wehāyāh laYHWH	He will belong to the Lord

Another of the phrases in the vow not elsewhere found with animals but only with people is *wehāyāh laYHWH* "he will belong to the Lord."[6] It is used, for example, for the consecration of the Levites to divine service, as in Numbers 3:12, when God says: *wehāyû lî hallewiyyīm* "the Levites shall be Mine." The classical prophets, especially Jeremiah, use the phrase a number of times to indicate the reconsecration of the Israelites back to God, for example, in Jeremiah 24:7: *wehāyû lî le'ām* "they will be My people," or Malachi 3:17: *wehāyû lî 'āmar YHWH ṣebā'ôt*, "they will be mine, said the Lord of Hosts."

Testimony of the Versions

The standard versions render the apodosis of the vow, for which the Hebrew has the double phrase *hayyôṣē' 'ašer yēṣē'* "whoever goes out," by only one phrase. The Targum appears to have interpreted one of the forms as an infinitive absolute since it renders *deyippôq mippaq*. Because the relative pronoun *de* is neutral, the phrase may be translated by "whoever" or "whatever will indeed go out" and could refer to animals as well as humans. Similarly, the LXX's rendering *ho ekporeuomenos* could be translated "whoever or whatever goes out," but the Peshitta and the Vulgate translations are more definitive. The Peshitta translates *man denāfēq* "whoever goes out" (not "whatever," which would be *mā denāfēq*), and the Vulgate renders *quicumque* "whoever" (not *quodcumque* "whatever").

Auxiliary Arguments

The auxiliary arguments presented here in support of the thesis that Jephthah originally intended an individual and not an animal are: (1) the vow was something special; (2) the vow was made in awareness of normal Israelite custom; (3) there was an inherent unlikelihood of an animal; (4) there was the possibility of an unclean animal.

The context shows that Jephthah intended to vow something special.[7] As has often been observed, vowing a sacrificial animal would not have promised anything especially significant.[8] On this point the 18th century scholar Augustus Pfeiffer is often quoted:[9] "What kind of vow would it be if some great prince or general should say, 'O God, if Thou will give me this victory, the first calf that meets me will be Thine'?"[10] It could no doubt be expected that without the vow Jephthah would have offered not one but many sacrifices after obtaining the victory. And, presumably, he would have offered the best of his flocks.[11]

It is reasonable to assume that Jephthah made his vow fully aware of the Israelite custom of maidens coming out to greet a victor after battle.[12] Jephthah's daughter indeed conformed to this custom by greeting her father, the victorious hero, with singing and dancing: "When Jephthah arrived at his home in Mizpah, there was his daughter coming out to meet him, with timbrel and dance!" (verse 34) The other examples of this Israelite custom are that of Miriam in Moses' time ("then Miriam the prophetess, Aaron's sister, took a timbrel in her hand and all the women went out after her in dance with timbrels"),[13] and that of the women in the time of Saul and David ("When the [troops] came home [and] David returned from killing the Philistines, the women of all the towns of Israel came out singing and dancing to greet King Saul with timbrels, shouting, and sistrums").[14] Therefore, in making his vow, Jephthah in all probability would have expected such a procession were he to return triumphant in battle. Thus he would have known that a human being would be leading the procession and would likely come out first to greet him.[15]

The phrase *yāṣā' liqrā't* "go out to greet" implies that the being going out be endowed with reason, intellect, and will.[16] It cannot, then, be seriously thought that a normally sacrificed domestic animal, such as a sheep or an ox, could *on its own accord* come out to greet anybody, even a general returning victoriously from war![17]

A further objection to the idea that the original intent of Jephthah's vow was that of an animal is the one which was initially raised by the earliest Rabbinical commentators. What if an animal that could not properly be sacrificed were to come out?

> Said the Holy One, blessed be He, to him: "Then had a camel, or a donkey, or a dog come out, would you have offered it up for an *'ôlāh*?[18]

Indeed, the only type of domestic animal that could possibly come out first ahead of human beings (a dog, a donkey, a horse, or a camel) was not permitted to be sacrificed.[19] According to Jewish tradition it was this fact alone that made Jephthah's vow illegitimate.[20]

Possibility of an Animal

A number of scholars are of the contrary opinion that the original intent of Jephthah was not a human being but an animal.[21] Numerous arguments are presented in favor of this point of view.

Kaufmann suggests that two of the phrases mentioned above, *daltê bayit* "doors of the house" and *yāṣā' liqrā't* "go out to greet," should not be taken literally. Jephthah's daughter obviously came out with singing and dancing at the head of a procession of women, certainly in the street or outside the city, far away from his house. The phrase *daltê bêtî* "doors of my house" has a much wider meaning and includes everything which belongs to Jephthah.[22] The phrase *yāṣā' liqrā't* means simply "to chance upon." Jephthah's intention was that he would sacrifice the first animal that belonged to him which he would meet.[23] Against these arguments are (a) the fact that the phrase *daltê bayit* elsewhere connotes the *inside* of a house, as, for example, in the Joshua passage previously mentioned: "if anyone ventures outside the doors of your house (*daltê bêtēk*)" (2:19), where there is a clear contrast between being inside the doors and *haḥûṣāh* "outside"; (b) if the phrase *daltê bayit* has the wider meaning of "estate," then the other people who would normally be on the estate, e.g., workers, bodyguards, bystanders, ought to be taken into consideration. It is hardly possible to think that the yard was empty as though, as one scholar put it, "they had all conspired to let his daughter come out first";[24] (c) there is no evidence that the phrase *yāṣā' liqrā't* means "to alight upon," "to chance upon."[25] This idea is normally expressed in Hebrew by a verb like *pg'*, as, for example, in Exodus 23:3, *kî tifga' šôr 'ōyibkā* "If you come across the ox of your enemy."

The second argument often raised by proponents of the animal theory is that parallel types of vows in other literatures show that the value of the offering was not in its weight or worth but on the fact that it was the first: whatever should be encountered first.[26] The best example for this motif is said to be found in the Greek legend of Idomenus as related by Servius, the ancient commentator on Virgil. Idomenus, king of Crete, was caught in a storm on his return home from the Trojan war. He vowed to Poseidon, god of the sea, that if he were saved he would sacrifice to him the first thing (*res*) that met him on his arrival home, which was his own son.[27] What is held to be most significant here is that Idomenus vows the first thing (*res*), not the first person. Indeed, Baumgartner has pointed out that in folklore vows of this nature, the father (making the vow) normally thinks of an animal, not of a human being (which it eventually turns out to be).[28]

However, it should be noted that there are a number of other stories of a similar type in which the father vows the first person, not the first thing. For example, in another Greek legend, Maeander vows that if he is granted victory in battle he will sacrifice the first person coming out to greet him on his return home.[29] Furthermore, it is of interest to observe that the Vulgate translation of Jephthah's vow includes the word *primus* ("first"), and it has already been noted that the Vulgate has in mind a person, since it uses the term *quicumque* "whoever." The Vulgate reads: "Whoever will come out first."[30]

So while the motif of the "first" is important, there is also evidence that this could be the first person, rather than the first thing or animal. This is in fact the view of a number of scholars: that Jephthah's vow was aimed at the *first* person who should come out,[31] presumably a household slave.[32]

In arguing against the original intent of the vow being a human being, Kaufmann points out that the only references to human sacrifices in the Bible, and in the entire Semitic world, are to child sacrifices.[33] Had the original intent, then, been a human being, one would have to assume that Jephthah, because he had only one child, intended from the very beginning to offer her up.[34] According to Kaufmann, the subsequent events of the story preclude this assumption, so that it is necessary to conclude that Jephthah really intended an animal.[35]

At first sight Kaufmann's argument seems to be strong, but it is based on the story's having an ending of literal sacrifice. A literal sacrifice, as this study demonstrates, is not at all certain. Furthermore, even if a child were usually the intended offering, it is not at all clear that Jephthah has his daughter in mind and not another child of his estate.

The strongest evidence that the original intent of the vow was an animal is in the phrase *weha'alîtīhû 'ôlāh* in the second part of the vow. The phrase *leha'alôt (le)'ôlāh* usually, though not exclusively, as the examples of Genesis 22:2 and 2 Kings 3:27 show, refers to animals. Furthermore, the suffix on *weha'alîtīhû* must refer back to the subject in the protasis of the vow, *hayyôṣē' 'ăšer yēṣē'*.[36] If this phrase does refer to an animal, then we have a situation where part of the vow would refer to a human being (*wehāyāh laYHWH*, see above p. 14), and another part (*weha'alîtīhû 'ôlāh*) would refer to an animal. This point was noticed by Jewish medieval commentators, and the Kimḥis used it as a basis for their theory that the vow was essentially disjunctive.[37] That is, it could refer to something inappropriate for sacrifice like an unclean animal (or a human being) [*wehāyāh laYHWH*], or to something appropriate for sacrifice like a clean animal [*weha'alîtīhû 'ôlāh*]. The *waw* before the phrase *weha'alîtīhû 'ôlāh* has to be taken as disjunctive "or," as is attested a number of times in the Hebrew Bible.[38] Thus, if the item that came out was not fitting for an *'ôlāh* it would be dedicated to the Lord (*wehāyāh laYHWH*), if it was fitting for an *'ôlāh*, it would be offered up as an *'ôlāh*. This view still has its adherents today.[39]

Against this interpretation is that for this line of argument to work, the phrases *wehāyāh laYHWH* and *weha'alîtīhû 'ôlāh* should be reversed. The emphasis is on whether the vowed object is fitting for the *'ôlāh* or not. The positive should precede the negative. Thus it should state: "(if it is fitting for an *'ôlāh*), I will offer it up, (but if it is not), he will belong to the Lord," not the reverse, as is in the text. Secondly, this would be the only example in ancient Semitic literature of a vow phrased in such a disjunctive "either . . . or" fashion.[40] Thirdly, if the *waw* is taken as disjunctive, it cannot have consecutive force, that is, the phrase *ha'alîtīhû 'ôlāh* cannot then have future meaning. Most scholars believe that there is no compelling reason why the phrase *weha'alîtīhû 'ôlāh* must refer to an animal, but, as the examples of Genesis 22:2 and 2 Kings 3:27 show, can be used with people. The *waw* conjunction is then taken as explicative: it explains what *wehāyāh laYHWH* "he shall belong to the Lord" means, namely, "he shall be offered up as an *'ôlāh*." Whether this *'ôlāh* is to be taken in a literal or figurative sense is a question which will be taken up later in this chapter.

Summary

My conclusion was stated at the outset: the weight of evidence seems to indicate that Jephthah intended to offer an individual, not an animal. Having said this, however, I propose a suggestion. It is possible, from the text as it now stands, that what appears is the first of a number of intentional ambiguities either by the original author or by the redactor. The reader or listener is not meant to know what the original intent really was. This feature is well known in folklore where language is chosen to be deliberately deceptive. In a story of this type, the father making the vow has something different in mind from what the deity or demon to whom he is vowing has.[41] The ambiguity heightens the tension of the entire story. Indeed there are some modern translators who maintain this ambiguity in their translations. For by translating the phrase *hayyôṣē' 'ašer yēṣē'* as "anything"[42] instead of "whoever," the reader does not know whether an animal or a human being is intended, and the suspense of the story is increased.[43] In any event, regardless of the original intent, whether Jephthah really meant an animal or an individual, his daughter subsequently was trapped in his vow.[44]

The question of how Jephthah's vow compares in structure with other vows found in the Hebrew Bible and the solitary one attested in Ugaritic literature is examined next. This is important because, as will be seen, the structure of a vow can often elucidate the vow's meaning.

STRUCTURE OF THE VOW

From a structural point of view, Jephthah's vow conforms in general to the four other examples of vows that are to be found in the Hebrew Bible (Jacob's vow in Genesis 28:20-22; Israel's vow in Numbers 21:2; Hannah's vow in 1 Samuel 1:11; and Absalom's vow in 2 Samuel 15:7-8). As can be seen from the following chart, the Jephthah vow shares with the others the following characteristics: (a) It is preceded in the introduction by the verb *ndr* and its cognate accusative (*yiddar Yiptaḥ neder*). (b) The deity to whom the vow is addressed is named (*laYHWH*).[45] (c) A form of the verb "to say" introduces the vow (here it is the pausal form of the *waw* consecutive, *wayyō'mar*). (d) A protasis, introduced by *'im*, which (except for Jacob's vow) contains an infinitive absolute plus the finite verb in the imperfect (*nātôn tittēn*). (e) An apodosis is expressed by the perfect consecutive (*wehāyāh, weha'alîtīhû*). However, there is one major difference. When the other four vows and the only extant vow from Ugarit are examined, it is noticeable that there is a parallelism in thought between the protasis and the apodosis. In all the cases there is a specific relation between the condition and what is promised,[46] indeed sometimes in exactly the same language. Thus, Jacob's promise to be God's devotee if He, God, will be with him (*'im yiheyeh 'elōhîm 'immādî* [protasis]; *wehāyāh YHWH lî lē'lōhîm* [apodosis]); Israel promises that if God delivers the Canaanites to them they will deliver them back (through devoting their cities) to God; Hannah vows that if she is given a male child she will give him back by consecrating him to God (*wenātattāh la'amāteka zera' 'anāšîm* [protasis], *ûnetattîw laYHWH kol yemê ḥayyâw* [apodosis]; Absalom promises to worship God if He will restore him back to Jerusalem from exile in Geshur; Keret promises the Goddess Asherah that if he is granted Ḥuraya as a wife he will give her weight in gold and silver (probably in the form of a statue) back to the deity.[47] Only in the Jephthah vow is there no direct relation between the condition and the promise.

The vow which is structurally and contextually the most similar to Jephthah's is the one of Israel. The protases of both are practically identical.

Jephthah	'im nātôn tittēn 'et benê 'ammôn beyādî
Israel	'im nātōn tittēn 'et hā'ām hazzeh beyādî

Hence, a similar apodosis, at least in thought, would, therefore, be expected: a restoration back to the deity of part of the defeated enemy as in the Israelite vow: *wehaḥaramtî 'et 'ārêhem* "I will utterly devote their towns." Instead Jephthah promises a person, completely unrelated to the condition of the vow, and more in line with Hannah's vow. In the lack of relation between the condition and the promise in Jephthah's vow, we must ask whether or not this is another deliberate attempt of the narrator to add to the general ambiguity of the entire passage.

The third group of major questions arising from verse 31 is examined next: the grammatical ones.

GRAMMATICAL QUESTIONS

As was already mentioned, the three grammatical questions arising from this verse are the following: (a) Why is there a double introductory formula? (b) Why is there an extra *wehāyāh* in the apodosis of the vow? (c) Is the phrase

Genesis 28:20-22 (Jacob's Vow)

Introduction	wayyiddar Ya'akōb nēdēr lē'mōr	Jacob then made a vow, saying,
Protasis	'im yiheyeh 'elōhîm 'immādî ûšemāranî badderek hazzeh 'ašer 'ānōkî hôlēk wenātan lî leḥem le'ekōl ûbeged lilbōš wešabtî bešālôm 'el bêt 'ābî	"If God remains with me, if He protects me on this journey that I am making, and gives me bread to eat and clothing to wear, and if I return safe to my father's house—
Apodosis	wehāyāh YHWH lî lē'lōhîm wehā'eben hazzō't 'ašer samtî maṣṣēbāh yihyeh bêt 'elōhîm wekōl 'ašer titten lî 'assēr 'a'asserennû lāk	The Lord shall be my God. And this stone, which I have set up as a pillar, shall be God's abode; and of all that You give me, I will always set aside a tithe for You."

Numbers 21:2 (Israel's vow)

Introduction	wayyiddar Yisrā'ēl neder laYHWH wayyō'mar	Then Israel made a vow to the Lord and said,
Protasis	'im nātōn tittēn 'et hā'ām hazzeh beyādî	"If You deliver this people into my hand,
Apodosis	wehaḥaramtî 'et 'ārêhem	I will utterly devote their towns."

Judges 11:30-31 (Jephthah's vow)

Introduction	wayyiddar Yiptaḥ neder laYHWH wayyō'mar	Then Jephthah made a vow to the Lord and said,
Protasis	'im nātōn tittēn 'et benê 'ammôn beyādî	"If you indeed deliver the Ammonites into my hands,
Apodosis	wehāyāh hayyôṣē' 'ašer yēṣē middaltê bêtî liqrātî bešûbî bešālôm mibbenê 'ammôn wehāyāh laYHWH weha'alî-tīhû 'ôlāh	Whoever comes out from the doors of my house to greet me, when I return safely from the Ammonites, will belong to the Lord, and I will offer him up as an *'ôlāh*.

1 Samuel 1:11 (Hannah's vow)

Introduction	wattiddōr neder wattō'mar	Then she made this vow:
Protasis	YHWH ṣebā'ôt 'im rā'ōh tir'eh bo'onî 'amāteka ûzekartānî welō' tiškaḥ 'et 'amātekā wenātattāh la'amātekā zera' 'anāšîm	"O Lord of Hosts, if You will look upon the suffering of Your maidservant and will remember me and not forget Your maidservant, and if You will grant Your maidservant a male child,
Apodosis	ûnetattîw laYHWH kol yemê ḥayyâw ûmôrāh lō' ya'aleh 'al rō'šô	I will dedicate him to the Lord for all the days of his life; and no razor shall ever touch his head."

2 Samuel 15:7-8 (Absalom's vow)

Introduction	'ēlekāh nā' wa'ašallēm 'et nidrî 'ašer nādartî laYHWH beḥebrôn kî nēder nādar 'abdekā bešibtî begešûr ba'arām lē'mōr	"Let me go to Hebron and fulfill a vow that I made to the Lord. For your servant made a vow when I lived in Geshur of Aram:
Protasis	'im yāšôb yešibēnî YHWH yerûšālaim	If the Lord ever brings me back to Jerusalem,
Apodosis	we'ābadetî 'et YHWH	I will worship the Lord."

I K, 1:199-206 (Keret's vow)

Introduction	ṯm yd[r K]rt ṯ' i iṯt Aṯrt Ṣrm wIlt Ṣdynm	There [Ke]ret the Noble vo[ws]: "As Asherah of Tyre exists, As Elath of Sidon!
Protasis	hm Ḥry bty iqḥ aš'rb ǵlmt ḥẓry	If Ḫuraya to my house I take, Bring the lass into my court,
Apodosis	ṯnh kspm atn wṯlṯh ḫrṣm	Her double I'll give in silver, And her treble in gold."

laYHWH misplaced in the verse? Should it not go with *'ôlāh* instead of *wehāyāh*?

Double Introductory Formula

It has already been observed above that at the beginning of the apodosis of the vow two expressions are used (*hayyôṣē'* and *'ašer yēṣē'*) which have identical meanings, when one would have been sufficient. It is commonly held that this is a dittography or an editorial gloss of sorts,[48] and that one or the other phrase should be omitted as is the case with all the standard versions (see above pp. 14-15).

Extra wehāyāh in the Apodosis

The form *wehāyāh* occurs once in the introduction to the first apodosis, *wehāyāh hayyôṣē' 'ašer yēṣē'* . . . "whoever goes out . . . will be," and once later on in the same apodosis, *wehāyāh laYHWH* "He will belong to the Lord."

wehāyāh hayyôṣē' 'ašer yēṣē' middaltê bêtî liqrā'tî bešûbî bešālôm mibbenê 'ammôn wehāyāh laYHWH weha'alîtīhû 'ôlāh

The sentence is usually analyzed as follows: the first *wehāyāh* "he will be" is the predicate; *hayyôṣē'* "whoever will go out" is the subject; the second *wehāyāh* is the predicate repeated; and *laYHWH* "to the Lord," is a prepositional phrase serving as the object. This means that the subject of the first *wehāyāh*, which is *hayyôṣē'* "whoever goes out," is interpreted as being the same as that of the second *wehāyāh*.[49]

The question must now be asked: is there any syntactic reason for the second *wehāyāh*? Without it, the sentence would be quite correct grammatically, since a reading *wehāyāh hayyôṣē'* . . . *laYHWH* would also obtain the meaning "whoever goes out . . . will belong to the Lord." Ehrlich has been the only commentator to see a difficulty here. He pointed out another example of a similar construction in Exodus 4:9 and suggested that the second *wehāyāh* is repeated due to the length of the sentence.[50] Exodus 4:9 reads as follows: *wehāyû hammayyim 'ašer tiqqaḥ min haYe'ōr wehāyû ledām bayyabāšet*, "the water that you have taken from the Nile will turn to blood on the dry ground." Here the form *wehāyû* is repeated, again apparently unnecessarily. Both sentences are illustrated below.

Object	Subject	Predicate	
[*wehāyāh*] *laYHWH*	*hayyôṣē' 'ašer yēṣē'*	*wehāyāh*	Judges 11:31
[*wehāyû*] *ledām*	*hammayim*	*wehāyû*	Exodus 4:9

While Ehrlich's suggestion certainly has merit, a comparison with other biblical constructions of this type indicates that something is lacking in the text. Thus, in an oath in Joshua 2:19, where the protasis is framed in language almost identical to Jephthah's vow: *wehāyāh kol 'ašer yēṣē' middaltê bêtēk haḥûṣāh*, "If anyone ventures outside the doors of your house," the apodosis reads: *dāmô berō'šô*, "his blood will be on his head." ["it is his own responsibility"]. The subject of the oath is clearly indicated in the term *dāmô* "his blood." Likewise, in another oath in 1 Samuel 17:25, a protasis introduced by *wehāyāh*—*wehāyāh hā'îš 'ašer yakkennû* "whoever kills him"—is concluded with *ya'šerennû hammelek 'ōšer gādôl* "the king will reward him with great riches." Once again the subject of the apodosis is unambiguously expressed. Furthermore, a perusal of the only other vow in the Hebrew Bible which has *wehāyāh* in the apodosis shows that something is missing in our apodosis, also introduced by *wehāyāh*. Jacob's vow in Genesis 28:20-22, "If God remains with me, if He protects me on this journey . . . " has the apodosis *wehāyāh YHWH lî lē'lōhîm* "the Lord shall be my God," where the subject of the vow "the Lord" is unequivocally denoted. This omission of the subject of Jephthah's vow in the apodosis cannot be lightly dismissed. It is present in the second part of Jephthah's vow, *weha'alîtīhû 'ôlāh* "I will offer him up as an *'ôlāh*," and in every one of the six vows in the Hebrew Bible and Ugaritic literature (see p. 20 above), including the only other vow of dedication, that of Hannah dedicating Samuel in 1 Samuel 1:11, where the apodosis reads, *ûnetattîw laYHWH kol yemê ḥayyâw* "I will dedicate him to the Lord for all the days of his life." Our text, then, should likewise have a subject expressed for the second *wehāyāh*, and one might expect a reading *wehāyāh laYHWH hû'*, or *hû' yiheyeh laYHWH*. Alternatively, since the second *wehāyāh* is syntactically unnecessary, and since a subject is otherwise expected with it, it is possible that some textual corruption has taken place with the following phrase *weha'alîtīhû 'ôlāh* "I will offer him up as an *'ôlāh*." This question will be examined next.

Textual Corruption in Last Part of the Verse

A problem arises because the phrase *weha'alîtīhû 'ôlāh* is not the norm in Hebrew. The expression "to offer something up as an *'ôlāh* should be rendered with the preposition *lamed* as, for example, in Genesis 22:13, *wayya'alēhû le'ôlāh taḥat benô* "He offered it up for an *'ôlāh* in place of his son."[51] Because of this linguistic problem, it has been suggested that the entire phrase is superfluous. Thus Boström believes that one apodosis, e.g., *wehāyāh laYHWH*, would have been sufficient; and since not a word is said about Jephthah's offering up a burnt offering when he fulfills his vow in verse 39, the phrase seems to be an obvious gloss, added when the story was no longer understood.[52] Were Boström's suggestion to be accepted, a major ambiguity would be removed, not only in terms of this verse but also in terms of the entire problem under discussion. But Boström's suggestion still does not resolve the problems connected with the phrase *wehāyāh laYHWH*. I believe that because in the phrase *wehāyāh laYHWH* the word *wehāyāh* is syntactically unnecessary and, strictly speaking, ought to have a subject accompanying it, and because in the phrase *weha'alîtīhû 'ôlāh* a preposition would be expected, some textual corruption has taken place. The word *laYHWH* originally belonged with the phrase *weha'alîtīhû 'ôlāh*, with the full phrase reading *weha'alîtīhû 'ôlāh laYHWH*. My suggestion is supported by the following facts: (a) the expression "to offer up an *'ôlāh* to the Lord" is most commonly rendered in Hebrew by *leha'alôt 'ôlāh laYHWH*;[53] (b) the Vulgate actually reads: *eum holocaustum offeram Domino* "I will offer him up as a burnt offering to the Lord"!

The omission of the phrase *laYHWH* may have been a deliberate act by the narrator or by a later editor to tone down the suggestion that Jephthah could indeed offer up a human sacrifice to Yahweh. Another passage where there may be an identical situation is in 2 Kings 3:27, in the oft-cited and well-known story of Mesha's sacrificing his firstborn son. The text reads:

> So he took his firstborn son, who was to succeed him as king, and offered him up on the wall as an *'ôlāh* (*wayya'alēhû 'ôlāh 'al haḥōmāh*).

We note that here too there is no preposition with the word *'ôlāh*. Indeed the absence of a preposition has led to a debate as to which deity the sacrifice was made: to Chemosh, the national god of Moab, or to Yahweh. I believe that it is quite possible that here too the phrase *laYHWH* has been deliberately omitted because it was considered unseemly to indicate that a human sacrifice might indeed be made to Yahweh. Ehrlich has observed that the efficacy of Mesha's sacrifice was dependent on his offering his son to Yahweh, not to Chemosh.[54] The great wrath that came upon Israel and forced her to retreat is only explicable if the sacrifice were offered to Yahweh. In the realpolitik of those times, Chemosh, as the losing god, was in no position to affect the situation even on his home territory.[55] It was only the victor god who could do that, and Yahweh, being the god of the allies, shows his anger at them by their being the cause of this unseemly sacrifice. It is interesting to note that the interpretation that Mesha offered his son to Yahweh, not to Chemosh, is to be found in various midrashim. For example, *Midrash Tanḥuma*, in commenting on the phrase *welō 'āletāh 'al libbî* "it did not occur to me" in Jeremiah 19:5 states:

> It did not occur to me: that the king of Moab would fall into the power of the king of Israel and he would offer to me his firstborn son, as it is said: "so he took his firstborn son . . . ." [2 Kings 3:27][56]

Summary

The observations on the grammatical questions in this verse may be summed up: (1) the double introductory formula *hayyôṣē'* and *'ašer yēṣē'* "whoever goes out" probably represents a dittography of sorts, and one or the other phrase should be omitted; (2) the second *wehāyāh* is syntactically unnecessary and, were it original, ought to have a subject; (3) the phrase *weha'alîtīhû 'ôlāh* is also grammatically exceptional because a preposition *lamed* is expected. Because of the last two arguments, it is reasonable to assume that some textual dislocation has taken place in the latter half of the verse, and my suggestion is to read it *weha'alîtīhû 'ôlāh laYHWH* "I will offer him up as an *'ôlāh* to the Lord." Nevertheless, whatever the original may have read, it must be acknowledged that the text as it now stands contains anomalous, though intelligible, Hebrew constructions.

These constructions would add admirable grist to the mill of any narrator desiring to have his story capable of having more than one meaning. When one adds matters which have previously been discussed, namely the ambivalence of the intention of the vow, the divergence in the structure of the vow, it is not at all surprising that the actual wording of the vow would be equally as equivocal: all contribute to the general ambiguity of the episode.

The final question in this verse concerns the meaning of the phrase *wehaʻalîtīhû ʻôlāh*, and in particular whether it can be interpreted in other than its literal meaning.

THE MEANING OF THE PHRASE *wehaʻalîtīhû ʻôlāh*

In some respects the phrase *wehaʻalîtīhû ʻôlāh* constitutes the crux of the entire problem under discussion. Were it to be removed (as suggested above by Boström) or reinterpreted in a non-literal meaning, it would radically affect the sacrificialists' point of view. As it stands, most scholars believe that the phrase should be taken literally. The term *ʻôlāh*, usually rendered by "burnt offering,"[57] is a technical one for a sacrifice wholly consumed by fire.[58] Jephthah vowed a literal sacrifice and fulfilled his vow by putting his daughter to death.[59] Some who favor a non-literal conclusion for the story maintain that the meaning of the phrase *wehaʻalîtīhû ʻôlāh* ought to be derived from the manner in which the vow was fulfilled. Inasmuch as there is no mention of a literal burnt offering when the vow is being fulfilled, it is argued that the phrase may have a modified meaning.[60] Impetus for such a modified interpretation is provided by the story of Samuel's consecration to divine service as related in the first chapter of 1 Samuel. Noting that when Samuel was consecrated an *ʻôlāh* was offered up at the same time,[61] symbolizing Samuel's complete dedication to divine service, it is posited that there is a correlation between consecration of people and offering up of *ʻôlôt*, with the latter symbolizing the former.

The suggestion, then, is that there is a feature in Jephthah's vow where alongside the promised consecration of an individual (*wehāyāh laYHWH*) is the offering of an *ʻôlāh*. On these lines two alternate theories have been put forward. The first takes the *ʻôlāh* to be a real *ʻôlāh* (an animal). The sense of the vow would then be: when I consecrate this individual I shall offer up an *ʻôlāh* which will symbolize the individual's complete consecration to God. However, such an interpretation necessitates translating the phrase *wehaʻalîtī-hû ʻôlāh* as "I will offer an *ʻôlāh* to Him,"[62] taking the suffix *hû* as dative. But elsewhere the dative for the verb *lehaʻalôt* is expressed with the preposition *l*.[63] So the suffix *hû*, as was mentioned above, must refer to the subject of the apodosis "the one going out," and can only be translated "I will offer him up."

The second theory is to take the phrase *wehaʻalîtīhû ʻôlāh* figuratively.[64] Just as the real *ʻôlāh* when offered up was offered up completely without anything remaining, so the person set apart as an *ʻôlāh* would be "offered up" completely to the Lord.[65] Jephthah's daughter had to remain a virgin for the remainder of her days.[66] The two phrases "He shall belong to the Lord" and "I will offer him up as an *'ôlāh*" would then be related to one another as genus and species. The first is a general statement, the second a particular one. Just as in Hannah's vow in 1 Samuel 1:11, "I will give him to the Lord," there is an additional phrase, "and no razor shall come upon his head," which elaborates on the type of dedication, e.g., he shall be a Nazarite, so also here, the second phrase elaborates the first. The second phrase, "I will offer him up as an *'ôlāh*," indicates how the vowed one is to be dedicated, and, taken figuratively, it means "to be dedicated wholly and exclusively."[67] Further, it is pointed out that there are passages in the Hebrew Bible where sacrifices are applied to people in a figurative sense. For example, in Numbers 8:11, 13 and 21, Aaron consecrates the Levites and designates them a *tenûfāh* "wave offering" before the Lord.

> Let Aaron designate the Levites before the Lord as a wave offering (*tenûfāh*) from the Israelites, that they may perform the service of the Lord. [v. 11]

> The Levites purified themselves and washed their clothes; and Aaron designated them as a wave offering before the Lord, and Aaron made expiation for them to cleanse them. [v. 21]

The intent here is purely symbolic.[68] The Levites are to be spiritual *tenûfāh*s. Likewise, it is alleged, Jephthah's daughter could have been a spiritual *'ôlāh* by dedicating her life to the Lord in lifelong chastity.[69]

The symbolic argument has strong support on two counts. The first is the fact that a literal *'ôlāh* is not mentioned in the fulfillment of the vow.[70] The second is the association of the *'ôlāh* and consecration in 1 Samuel. Against it are two arguments that are just as strong, if not stronger. The first is that nowhere else in the Hebrew Bible is *'ôlāh* used figuratively,[71] especially in the other two cases involving human beings in Genesis 22 and 2 Kings 3. Secondly, the symbolic interpretation requires acceptance of the unlikely fact of the existence of two phrases occurring side by side, one being literal ("he will belong to the Lord") and the other figurative ("I will offer him up as an *'ôlāh*).[72] Once again doubt remains. It should not by now be a surprise that this may in fact have been the original intent of the narrator. In the light of all the other intentional ambiguities which we have posited for this verse, the narrator may have wanted to leave it to the reader to decide whether or not literal or figurative sacrifice is meant here.

SUMMARY

The conclusions concerning the questions arising from verse 31 may be summarized as follows: (1) The weight of evidence seems to indicate that Jephthah intended to offer an individual, not an animal. (2) In examining the structure of Jephthah's vow in comparison to other vows, it can be seen that there is no direct relation between the condition and the promise. Jephthah offers a person instead of part of the defeated enemy as might have been expected. (3) The Hebrew text as it now stands contains some anomalous constructions, and probably some textual dislocation has occurred. The present text speaks both of consecrating an individual to God and of offering him up as an *'ôlāh*. (4) There is perhaps more weight to the argument that the phrase "I will offer him up as an *'ôlāh*" be taken literally rather than figuratively, though the latter is not wholly excluded.

Having discussed questions arising from the making of the vow itself, I now turn to questions arising from the daughter's involvement in the vow which are related in verses 34-38. These questions are the subject of chapter 2.

THE DAUGHTER'S INVOLVEMENT: VERSES 34-38

The Daughter Was Jephthah's Only Child

The vow having been made, Jephthah goes to battle against the Ammonites. The narrator spends little time on the details of the battle, but indicates in a few deft strokes that Jephthah has completely routed his enemies and emerged victorious. It is now time for Jephthah to return home to receive the acclaim of his countrymen. As he approaches home, his daughter, apparently unaware of the vow he made in the field of battle,[1] comes out to greet him in accord with the custom of maidens welcoming home heroes.[2] Thus she gets caught in Jephthah's vow. The text reads:

> His daughter came out to greet him with timbrels and dancing. She was an only child (*weraq hî' yeḥîdāh*); he had no other son or daughter (*'ên lô mimmennû* [*qerê: mimmennāh*][3] *bēn 'ô bat*).

The question has sometimes been raised about the status of Jephthah's daughter; was she really Jephthah's only child? Some Jewish medieval commentators (Kimḥi and Abravanel), and some moderns (Ehrlich and Zapletal) have posited the thesis that the daughter was not Jephthah's only child, but that he had others as well.

Thus David Kimḥi, retaining the *ketîb mimmennû* "from him" in the phrase "there was not from him any son or daughter," comments:

> It is possible that Jephthah's wife had children from a former marriage and that Jephthah had adopted them as his own. But he only had one natural child—this daughter.[4]

Ehrlich and Zapletal prefer reading the *qerê*: *mimmennāh* "from her" and translate "compared to her, there existed for him no other of his children."[5] That is, she was such a favorite for him that it seemed as if the other children did not exist. In support of their thesis Ehrlich and Zapletal make two points: (1) Jephthah's daughter is termed a *yeḥîdāh*, the same word used to describe Isaac in Genesis 22:2. Because Abraham had another son, *yeḥîd*(*āh*) cannot mean an "only" child, rather a "favorite" or "beloved" child.[6] (2) In an age when Jephthah's immediate predecessor, Yair, had 30 sons (and just before him Gideon, who had 70 sons), and Jephthah's immediate successor, Ibzan, had 60 children, it would be unlikely for a man like Jephthah to have had only one child, and a daughter at that!

In defense of the commonly accepted interpretation that Jephthah's daughter was his sole child the following points may be made: (1) The presence of the adverb *raq* "only" makes the Hebrew "extraordinarily emphatic";[7] it literally means "she only was a *yeḥîdāh*." With the adverb, translating *yeḥîdāh* as "favorite" or "beloved" just does not work: "she was only a favorite child." The traditional "she was absolutely an only child"[8] is by far to be preferred. (2) The fact that Jephthah's immediate predecessors and successors had numerous progeny as compared to Jephthah's solitary one only serves to highlight and emphasize the severity of Jephthah's sacrifice.[9]

Why Jephthah Mourned

The appearance of his daughter causes Jephthah great grief: he rends his clothes—the traditional sign of mourning—as he realizes that she has become involved in his vow:

> On seeing her, he rent his clothes and said, "Alas daughter! You have brought me low: you have become my troubler! For I have uttered a vow to the Lord and I cannot retract." [verse 35]

Why does Jephthah mourn? According to the sacrificialists, because his only daughter is now to die.[10] According to the non-sacrificialists, because she has to remain celibate for life.[11]

Whichever point of view one follows, the consequence for Jephthah will be the same: the end of his line, the termination of the clan of Jephthah himself.[12] Regardless of the daughter's ultimate fate, whether she is actually sacrificed or consecrated as a perpetual virgin, in either case she is going to die unmarried and childless,[13] hence Jephthah's grief.[14]

Both Jephthah and his daughter represent the point of view, common among the Israelites, that a vow is a sacred obligation which must be fulfilled under all circumstances.[15] Jephthah says: "for I have uttered a vow to the Lord and I cannot retract" (verse 35), which the daughter echoes in: "'Father,' she said, 'You have uttered a vow to the Lord; do to me as you have vowed'" (verse 36). But the daughter also connects her fate with that of her people by adding, "since the Lord has vindicated you against your enemies." Thus she comprehends that the victory in battle, which was vowed for and ultimately granted her father, had to be paid for by a sacrifice on her part.

It is noteworthy that nobody attempts to save the daughter. Not Jephthah, who, according to Jewish tradition, could have saved her had he not been engaged in a bitter dispute with the then high priest, Phineas.[16] Nor the people, who later will intercede and save Jonathan when Saul condemns him to death as a result of an equally rash oath.[17] It was as though it was thought that if God had delivered the daughter to Jephthah it was a sign that He wished the girl for Himself.[18]

The Daughter's Request

The daughter's only request is a respite of two months to go to the hills with her friends and "mourn her virginity";

> She said to her father, "Let this thing be allowed me; let me alone [*harpēh mimmennî*] for two months, that I may go [*we'ēlekāh*] and wander [*weyāradtî*] on the hills and bewail my virginity [*we'ebkeh 'al betûlay*], I and my dear friends [*'anōkî werē'ôtāy*]. So he said to her, "Go!" He sent her for two months. She and her friends went [*wattēlēk*] and bewailed [*wattēbk*] her virginity, [*'al betûleyhā*] away on the hilltops [verses 37 and 38].[19]

The meaning of the three details in the daughter's request are not very clear at all, and have given rise to numerous interpretations on the following questions: (1) What is the significance of the two months? (2) Why does she wish to go to the hills? (3) What does the phrase "to bewail my virginity" mean?

THE SIGNIFICANCE OF THE TWO MONTHS

The significance of the two months requested by the daughter has never been satisfactorily explained. The number two has no bearing on the festival, later to be described, because that festival is to last four (not two) days a year. However, both sacrificialists and non-sacrificialists use this detail as an argument against the other side's conclusions. The sacrificialists argue that were Jephthah's daughter going to live a life of virginity, she would not need an initial period of two months to bewail her virginity; she would have plenty of time for that later.[20] The non-sacrificialists contend that, were death an issue, it would be against human nature for a devoted daughter about to die not to want to spend the last days of her life with her father, but instead insist on going to the hills for two months.[21]

Reason for Wanting to go to the Hills

The Hebrew text describing the daughter's request to go to the hills contains one of the two well-known textual cruxes in the entire chapter.[22] The phrase *weyāradtî 'al hehārîm* lit. "I will go down on the hills" is difficult both contextually and syntactically. It is difficult contextually because, as has often been pointed out, only God can descend on the hills.[23] As for syntax, H. M. Orlinsky has demonstrated that the form *weyāradtî*, occurring as it does after the forms *harpēh* "leave me," *we'ēlekāh* "let me go," and before *we'ebkeh* "let me weep," is grammatically odd. A perfect with a *waw* consecutive (*weyarād-tî*) is never found in a sequence between an imperative (*harpēh*), a cohortative (*ēlekāh*) and a following cohortative (*we'ebkeh*). What would be expected is another cohortative (*we'ēredāh* "let me go down"), or that the other forms after the imperative should be perfects with *waw* consecutive (e.g., *wehalaktî*, *webakîtî*).[24] Orlinsky, following the suggestion of Margolis,[25] takes *weyarādtî* as a dittography and corruption of the form *werē'ôtî* "my friends," and suggests it ought to be omitted,[26] especially since the verb (*yrd*) is not mentioned in the sequel in verse 38 when the daughter goes (*wattēlēk*) and laments (*wattēbk*) on the mountains. Many other suggestions have been made regarding the form *weyarādtî*, some taking it from a different root and others emending it.[27] But whatever the precise meaning is, or even if (as suggested above) it does not belong in the verse, the sense of the passage is clear: the daughter desires to go away to the hills. The question to consider now is why. Some believe that she went to the hills for help. Thus the Midrash speaks of the daughter consulting the Sanhedrin[28] or the elders.[29] Tur-Sinai believes she wanted to seek divine assistance,[30] and Mahalman posits Ashtoreth and Baal as the gods to whom she prayed.[31]

It may be observed here that in classical mythology the virgin goddess Artemis had her residence on the mountains. It is considered fitting by some scholars that the daughter should lament her virginity in the home of the great virgin goddess.[32]

Some non-sacrificialists believe that she wanted to go to the hills because this was a place of solitude; very appropriate for a maid, in the company of her friends and away from male company, to lament over not being able to experience the joys of physical love.[33] Thus Cassel remarks: "The mountains are the abode of a pure and elevated solitude, in which her own chaste heart and those of her companions can open themselves without being overheard."[34]

Another possibility is that the emphasis in the story is not the hills at all but the fact that she is to go away with her friends.[35] The suggestion is that since she will be spending the rest of her life in seclusion she will not be able to be with her friends anymore. Indeed, there is a Jewish tradition that the four days of the festival, to be described later, were the only times in the year that she could have company. On these days the girls used to come and console her.[36]

Meaning of the Phrase "to bewail her virginity"

The phrase *libkôt 'al betûleyhā* "to bewail her virginity" is understood by the sacrificialists as meaning that the daughter is going to die a virgin.[37] Hence, she will die unmarried and childless,[38] considered a terrible fate for a woman in Israel.[39] The daughter is, thus, like Antigone, holding her own death lamentation.[40] Moreover, parallels are shown from early Greek myths that a human victim nearly always is a virgin.[41] The non-sacrificialists point out that not a word is mentioned in the text that she is lamenting her young life.[42] The phrase "to bewail her virginity" does not mean she is going to die.[43] The word *betûlîm* does not mean "youth,"[44] nor "maidenhood,"[45] but "the condition of virginity."[46] If sacrifice were intended, why should she only bewail her virginity? She would bewail her life.[47] Furthermore, Cassel notes: "A person expecting death and ready for it, would ask no time for lamentation. Such a one dies, and is lamented by others."[48] The non-sacrificialists maintain that it is not her early death that she is lamenting. On the contrary, she is lamenting the fact that she has to *live* and remain a virgin for the rest of her life.[49] The emphasis in the text is not on her premature death but on her virginity. Because of the fact that there is mention of her virginity three times both before and after the fulfillment of the vow, it is held by this school that her virginity is in fact the offering. Her lifelong virginity, with its concurrent childlessness, is what results after her father fulfills his vow.[50] Moreover, this school can also point to parallels from classical sources involving virgins by adducing the motif of virgins weeping because they remain unmarried.[51]

It is interesting to note at this point the interpretation of Boström, who also believes that her virginity is the offering. However, he observes that "we only bewail that which we lose, or are going to lose," so that the phrase "to bewail her virginity" means exactly that: she is going to lose her virginity. Jephthah's daughter was to be dedicated to the deity as a hierodule or sacred prostitute.[52]

SUMMARY

In summing up the observations on the various questions dealing with the daughter's involvement in Jephthah's vow, I highlight the following: Jephthah mourns because the consequence of his vow will mean that his line will end.

His only (and according to some, his only natural) daughter is to be put to death or be consecrated to God. In either case, she will die childless. The daughter requests a respite of two months to go to the hills to lament her virginity. The significance of these details is debated by both sacrificialists and non-sacrificialists. Neither side can offer anything plausible for the two months. The sacrificialists interpret the expression "to bewail her virginity" in a figurative sense as meaning bewailing her untimely death. The non-sacrificialists, taking the expression literally, believe that the details of the daughter's request must represent things (like going to the hills with her friends) that she will be unable to do later when she commences her celibate life.

After surveying questions concerning the daughter's involvement in Jephthah's vow, I examine in the next chapter verses 39 and 40, which relate how the vow was actually fulfilled and what happened afterwards.

THE FULFILLMENT AND THE AFTERMATH: VERSES 39-40

The fulfillment and the aftermath of the vow are described in verses 39-40:

> After two months' time, she returned to her father, and he did to her as he had vowed. She had never known a man / She did not know a man. So it became a custom in Israel / So she became an example in Israel. The Israelite maidens would go every year, for four days in the year, to mourn for / to celebrate the daughter of Jephthah the Gileadite.

As can be seen from the variants in our translation, these verses contain a number of questions; the three principal ones are: (1) Is the Hebrew phrase *wehîʾ lōʾ yādeʿāh ʾîš* to be taken as circumstantial "she had never known a man" or as consequential "she did not know a man"? (2) Should the Hebrew phrase *watehî ḥōq beyisrāʾēl* be interpreted as "it became a custom in Israel" or as "she became an example in Israel"? (3) What is the nature of the annual festival: one of mourning or of celebration?

Whether the Phrase *wehîʾ lōʾ yādeʿāh ʾîš* is Circumstantial or Consequential

Because the phrase *wehîʾ lōʾ yādeʿāh ʾîš* follows immediately after the statement "he did to her as he vowed," it has occupied a central place in the debate over the fate of Jephthah's daughter. The nature of the fulfillment of the vow has, of course, direct bearing on the vow itself, because it is thought that the real sense of the vow may be determined by the way it was carried out.[1] Thus much has been written about the meaning of this phrase, whether it actually reflects the fulfillment of the vow (what happened to the daughter), or simply describes the condition of the daughter when Jephthah put his vow into effect. It is obvious that the correct syntactical interpretation of this phrase is of the utmost importance, and there are two ways of interpreting the syntax.

Because of the presence of the personal pronoun *hîʾ*, most scholars (and hence the sacrificialists) interpret the phrase circumstantially.[2] As a circumstantial clause the phrase *wehîʾ lōʾ yādeʿāh ʾîš* is to be translated "and she not having known a man" or "she had not known a man." Thus Boling's translation is typical: "He fulfilled with her the vow which he had made. She had never had intercourse with a man."[3] Taken this way, the clause is merely a statement about the condition of Jephthah's daughter at the time of her death, that is, she died a virgin. In fact, the New English Bible translates it this way: "she died a virgin."[4] The sacrifice is held by this fact to be so much the greater.[5]

The alternative explanation adopted by the non-sacrificialists is that the phrase is consequential. This school holds that it is unlikely that this phrase would be a circumstantial clause describing the chastity of the daughter at the time of the fulfillment of the vow inasmuch as it is already known from a previous verse that she was a virgin. A statement to that effect now would contribute nothing new to the story.[6] Accordingly, it is held that the phrase should be taken as an independent clause with the personal pronoun *hî'* being used for emphasis.[7] In this way, the clause is interpreted as consequential. Taking the clause consequentially, it is translated "she did not know any man." This represents the consequence of the preceding "he did to her as he had vowed."[8] As a result of Jephthah's vow, she did not know any man. The consequence of his vow was that she lived a life of virginity.[9]

"It Became a Custom in Israel" or "She Became an Example in Israel"

The phrase *watehî ḥōq beyisrā'ēl*, when rendered "it became a custom in Israel," is usually joined to the following verse 40, yielding the following translation: "So it became a custom for the maidens of Israel to go every year, for four days in the year . . . ."[10] But this translation necessitates emending the text because: (a) there is an incongruence between the noun *ḥōq* "custom," which is masculine, and *watehî* "it became," which is feminine; (b) the idiom "to be a custom" needs a preposition *lamed*, either before *ḥōq* as, for example, in 1 Samuel 30:25, *wayesimehā leḥōq ulemišpāṭ leyisrā'ēl* "It was made a fixed rule for Israel,"[11] or after *ḥōq* as, for example, in Psalms 81:5, *kî ḥōq leyisrā-'ēl hû'* "For it is a law for Israel."[12]

Most scholars have resorted to emending the text by inserting the missing *lamed*, and either taking *watehî* as impersonal,[13] or emending it to *wayehî*, e.g., *wayehî leḥōq*.[14] However, the phrase as it stands means "she became a *ḥōq* in Israel." What *ḥōq* exactly means here is difficult to say. Certainly the regular meanings "statute," "ordinance," "decree," etc.[15] will not fit here. A hint may be found in the Peshitta's rendering of *ḥōq* by *'etā'*, a word normally used to translate the Hebrew words *'ôt*, *môpēt*, *nēs*, "sign," "symbol," "token," "standard," but also having the additional meaning of "example" or "model."[16] Thus, the Syriac may be rendered, "she became an example in Israel."[17] In favor of taking *watehî* in its literal sense, "and she became" is not only the admittedly late verse division but also the presence of the preceding *wehî'*, which forms a stylistic sequence of the feminine pronoun *hî'* and the feminine verb *watehî*. The same sequence is found once again in Ezekiel 19:14, *qînāh hî' watehî leqînāh* "this is a dirge, and it has become a [familiar] dirge."[18] If the phrase be interpreted in this manner, the question remains: of what or for what did she become this example or model? Was it because she voluntarily remained celibate, or because she voluntarily elected to die? This is yet another ambiguity to add to the growing list.

The Annual Festival

The nature of the annual festival said to be celebrated for Jephthah's daughter by the Israelite maidens for four days every year is decidedly unclear. It is not certain what type of festival it was, whether one of mourning or not.

Part of the ambiguity arises because of difficulties in interpreting the verb *letannôt*, which is used in verse 40 to describe the main activity of the festival. The various interpretations offered for this verb will first be discussed, and then the various theories offered for the origin and nature of this festival will be surveyed.

Interpretations of the Verb letannôt

On the basis of the LXX translation *threnein*, the verb *letannôt* is customarily rendered "to mourn."[19] Hence Boling: "It became a custom, year after year, that the daughters of Israel should go to mourn for the daughter of Jephthah the Gileadite, four days each year."[20] Because of this translation, some scholars have maintained that the annual festival involving Jephthah's daughter was one to do with mourning, especially those who try to explain the festival on mythological grounds like weeping for Tammuz or other gods.[21] Added to this is the fact that Jephthah's daughter would have died a virgin and childless, which, as noted before, was considered a terrible fate for a woman in Israel.[22] Sacrificialists and non-sacrificialists alike point to this translation as proof of the correctness of their respective positions.

The sacrificialists claim that the annual festival of mourning could have no basis unless the daughter were actually killed.[23] The non-sacrificialists believe that the maidens were mourning the fact that Jephthah's daughter, in volunteering to remain celibate, could not marry and have children.[24] There is here a measure of agreement on both sides. Because of the remarkable event which occurred, Jephthah's daughter could not have any children. One side believes it was because she died; the other because she had to remain celibate.

On the basis of its only other occurrence in the Hebrew Bible, in Judges 5:11, it is claimed that *letannôt* cannot mean "to mourn," because this meaning would not fit the context of the Judges 5 passage, which requires a meaning such as "to celebrate," "to recount." The passage reads: "There let them retell (*yetannû*) Yahweh's victories, victories by his own prowess in Israel." Thus, there is really no reason why the verb could not have this meaning in the Jephthah passage as well. As with the "mourning" interpretation, so with this "celebration" one; both sides can find a reason why this particular translation would suit their point of view best. The festival simply commemorates the fate of Jephthah's daughter, whatever that may have been: according to the sacrificialists, it was her death;[25] according to the non-sacrificialists, her voluntary celibacy.[26]

Another interpretation of *letannôt* as "to talk to" or "to console" can be found in the commentaries of the Jewish medievals David Kimḥi, Ralbag (Levi ben Gershom), and Abravanel.[27] According to them, the events described in verse 40 do not represent a festival at all, but actual events in the lifetime of the daughter. This interpretation, of course, is dependent on acceptance of an ending for the story that Jephthah's daughter went into seclusion. She was only permitted company four times a year, and it was then the maidens would come and either "talk to" her, or "console" her.

In accordance with his theory that the annual festival was one in which the maids offered their virginity, Boström proposed that the form *letannôt* is a denominative from *'etnāh* "fee for prostitution" (Hosea 2:14; 9:1), and means "to prostitute."[28] But, if the maids are prostituting themselves, then a reflexive form, such as a *hithpael*, is required, instead of the *piel* currently in the text.

Of the four theories, the first two, "to mourn" and "to celebrate," are the ones principally accepted. Neither meaning really helps elucidate what actually happened to Jephthah's daughter. There is no doubt that the festival commemorated a unique and remarkable event, but was this event voluntary celibacy or human sacrifice? As will be demonstrated in the next chapter, neither voluntary celibacy for women nor human sacrifice was the norm in Israel. Hence, either of these events could have occasioned an annual festival of commemoration. Thus, Cassel remarks in advocating the celibacy conclusion: "The history of Jephthah's daughter is related as something extraordinary. Her virginity must remain intact. On this account she is lamented, and a festival celebrated for her sake."[29] De Vaux, advocating a literal sacrifice, comments: "The fact that it [the sacrifice] was commemorated serves to stress how much such a sacrifice was considered extraordinary."[30]

Meaning of the Festival

The majority of scholars today believe that the story about Jephthah's daughter is etiological.[31] It is believed that there was in Israel a festival in which the maidens participated for four days, and this story was told to explain how the festival came into existence. Although there is no trace of this festival anywhere else in the Bible, quite a number of suggestions have been made concerning its origin and nature.[32] Some have posited a mythological basis for the festival: it originated from a ceremony of lament for the death of Tammuz, Baal, Osiris, or some other deity.[33] Others have suggested that the ceremony was based on fertility rites.[34] In both cases the religious ritual would have been given a historical explanation by the Jephthah story.[35]

As to the nature of the festival, one scholar holds that since there is an emphasis in the text on the daughter's lamenting her virginity, the festival may have been a pre-nuptial ceremony for girls on the threshold of marriage, who would be lamenting their impending loss of virginity.[36] Another scholar maintains the exact opposite, that it was for girls who are not yet married, and are lamenting the fact that they are still virgins.[37] Still another believes that the festival was one in which virgins had to prostitute themselves in a ritual ceremony.[38]

Because there is no mention of this festival anywhere else in the Bible, a number of scholars believe that the festival is not etiological, that the story of Jephthah and his daughter was told for reasons other than to explain the festival.[39] It ought to be observed that none of the etiological theories adequately explains how the four days of the festival tie in with the story which speaks of two months.[40] Nor do we know whether the four days were consecutive or spread out over the year.

SUMMARY

In this chapter, three more expressions are encountered that are capable of more than one interpretation. Two of these expressions have bearing on the question of the fate of Jephthah's daughter. The phrase *wehî' lō' yādeʻāh 'îš* is of critical importance because if it is taken circumstantially, it favors the sacrificial point of view, while if it is taken consequentially, it helps immeasurably the non-sacrificial point of view. The nature of the annual festival is uncertain because of the ambiguity regarding the interpretation of the verb *letannôt*. It is simply not known whether the festival described in verse 40 was one of mourning or of a different nature. Both sides have used the two major translations, "to mourn" and "to celebrate," to bolster their claims to their respective conclusions: voluntary celibacy or human sacrifice. The majority of scholars believe that the festival is etiological, but a good case can be made for the opposing point of view, particularly because there is no record anywhere else of this festival in ancient Israel.

The last three chapters have surveyed textual and exegetical questions arising from the story of Jephthah and his vow as presented in chapter 11 of the Book of Judges. In the next chapter, the external evidence which has been raised to elucidate the story shall be evaluated. This includes other biblical evidence, as well as correspondences with similar motifs in outside literatures.

EXTERNAL CONSIDERATIONS

In this chapter, the external evidence which has been brought to shed light on the Jephthah story will be discussed. Parallels have been shown with the story of Abraham and Isaac in Genesis 22; correspondence has been indicated with motifs in other literatures; evidence has been brought for and against celibacy of women in Israel; and, lastly, much debate has centered on whether the story of Jephthah's daughter represents one of the rare examples of human sacrifice in Israel. All the above have been used by one side or the other to bolster their points of view concerning the fate of Jephthah's daughter. It is necessary to see whether or not these parallels can aid us in elucidating the conclusion of the Jephthah story; the parallels adduced between the story and that of Abraham and Isaac in Genesis 22 will be considered first.

Parallels with Genesis 22

Similarities

The most obvious parallel between the Jephthah story and Genesis 22 is that in both stories fathers are prepared to sacrifice their children, literally or figuratively. Secondly, a similar terminology is employed: both Isaac and Jephthah's daughter are termed *yeḥîd(āh)* "only child," and both stories use the phrase *leha'alôt (le)'ôlāh* "to offer up as an *'ôlāh*." Using structural analysis, Edmund Leach has observed that, beyond the slight similarity in content, both stories appear to have an identical, though reverse, structure.[1] He charted the sequence of events in both stories as follows:

JEPHTHAH	*ABRAHAM AND ISAAC*
a. Jephthah makes a vow to make a burnt offering to God if he is granted victory.	d. God requires Abraham to sacrifice his only son Isaac as evidence of faith and obedience.
b. God grants Jephthah victory.	c. As Abraham prepares to obey, God imposes a substitution whereby Abraham in fact sacrifices an animal in fulfillment of his duty.
c. By implication Jephthah plans to sacrifice an animal or a slave in fulfillment of his vow.	b. Abraham thus demonstrates his faith and obedience.
d. God, in the form of chance, imposes a substitution whereby Jephthah is made to sacrifice his only child, a virgin daughter.	a. God makes a vow that Abraham shall have countless descendants.
OUTCOME	
Jephthah has no descendants of any kind.	All the children of Israel claim descent from Abraham.

Leach pointed out that, when presented in this way, the two stories appear as mirror images of each other:

> "God" is changed to "father", "father" is changed to "God", "virgin daughter" is changed to "virgin son"; the sequence represented by the clauses (a), (b), (c), (d) in the first story is exactly reversed in the second story. The mythical outcome of the first story "the father has

> no descendants" is the exact opposite of the mythical outcome of the second "the father has countless descendants."[2]

According to Leach, then, these two stories have an identical structure.

Differences

Five principal differences have been noticed between the two stories. As far as externals are concerned, Abraham's son is named but Jephthah's daughter is not.[3] Isaac comes from a "good family," a respectable family lineage; the daughter in the Jephthah story has a father of illegitimate birth and her mother is never mentioned.[4] In the Genesis story, God is testing Abraham's faith. In contrast, Jephthah, by attempting to ensure his victory via his vow, is in fact testing God.[5] Abraham passes the test and so is ensured descendants; Jephthah's lack of faith leads to an outcome where he has no descendants. Jephthah does not offer his daughter any comfort or possibility of release.[6] On the other hand, Abraham displays compassion toward Isaac by assuring him, albeit evasively, that "God will provide the sheep for His burnt offering, my son" (Genesis 22:8). As Trible has noted: "Unlike the father Abraham, Jephthah fails to evoke the freedom of the deity to avert disaster."[7] No divine messenger comes at the last instant to deliver Jephthah's daughter.[8] The elliptical manner in which the narrator reports Jephthah carrying out his vow, "he did to her as he had vowed" (verse 39), contrasts greatly with the story of Abraham and Isaac where attention is placed on all the details: the building of the altar, the laying out of the wood, the binding of Isaac, the laying him on the altar, the picking up of the knife—all building to incredible suspense.[9]

Implication of the Parallels

Can any of these parallels help in clarifying the conclusion of the Jephthah story? Three of them have some bearing on the fate of Jephthah's daughter. It might be supposed that were the Jephthah story structurally the mirror image of the Isaac story, then, inasmuch as Isaac is not sacrificed, the reverse should mean that Jephthah's daughter is. But, even if this is granted, the problem remains as to the nature of the "sacrifice": is it literal or figurative? The outcome of the story will be exactly the same whether Jephthah's daughter was actually sacrificed or not: he will not have any descendants by either conclusion.

Does the fact that an angel intervenes in the Isaac story but not in the Jephthah story mean, as some believe,[10] that the daughter was actually sacrificed? Not necessarily so, because if, as the non-sacrificialists contend, she is to remain a life-long virgin, or be dedicated to God's service, there would be no need for such divine intervention.

What about the elliptical manner in which it is recorded how Jephthah carried out his vow? It has often been alleged that this fact indicates how the narrator casts a veil over the final act to spare the reader the details;[11] the narrator "spares us the suspense and agony of details."[12] Thus the assumption is that all the suspense in the Isaac story, created by the attention to the details, is bearable because Isaac is to be spared; hence the corresponding lack of details in the Jephthah story means that the daughter is not spared: "though the son was saved, the daughter is slain."[13] But how valid is this assumption? Can one assume a direct literary relationship between two different authors bearing two entirely different messages? What does it mean that the narrator does not supply all the details here? He does not spare the reader the agony of details elsewhere in the Book of Judges, when relating, for example, the executions of Eglon or Siserah. Why would he not describe the sacrifice of Jephthah's daughter if she were indeed sacrificed? Indeed, an argument can be made for the opposite conclusion. The narrator, who normally gives details of executions, does not give the details here because there was no execution. The detail which is given is in fact what actually happened: "she did not know a man," i.e., she was dedicated to life-long virginity.

In sum, the parallels between the story of Abraham and Isaac and that of Jephthah and his daughter cannot be used with any conviction by either side to bolster conclusions concerning the fate of Jephthah's daughter.

THE MOTIFS IN OTHER LITERATURES

The first task in considering parallels to the Jephthah story in other literatures is to correctly identify the motifs which will be the subject for comparison. In spite of the fact that some parts of the Jephthah story are, in my opinion, ambiguous, three motifs which pertain to the vow can be identified with reasonable certainty. These are the motif of vowing to a deity as a consideration for delivery from some distress or for success in battle; the motif of vowing to sacrifice the first thing or person; the motif that as a result of a rash vow a beloved or only child is sacrificed. Whether the sacrifice is carried out literally or figuratively is a question that will be left in abeyance for the moment.

The Three Motifs in Different Stories

All of the above motifs are reasonably well documented in other literatures and folklore.[14] One example for each must suffice here.

(From China) A military officer from the city of Ke-sat, before going out to war, vowed to sacrifice his daughter to an idol. He was successful in battle, but did not wish to sacrifice his daughter. His ship was stopped, making it impossible for him to pass, and he was forced to drown his daughter. The inhabitants of the city then honored the daughter as their tutelar spirit.[15]

(From Arabia) Al Mundaḥir made a vow that on a certain day in each year he would sacrifice the first person he saw. His favorite poet Abid came in sight on the unlucky day, and was accordingly killed and the altar smeared with his blood.[16]

(From classical mythology) Agamemnon vowed to Artemis to sacrifice to her the most beautiful creature born that year within his realm. It so happened that the most beautiful thing born that year was his own daughter Iphigenia. He delayed the sacrifice until one day when he was forced to comply to effectuate the release of his ships grounded for weeks at Aulis. The prophet Calchas had announced that only with Iphigenia's sacrifice would Artemis grant a favorable wind:

> Agamemnon, Captain of Hellas, there can be no way of setting your ships free, till the offering you promised Artemis is given Her. You had vowed to render Her in sacrifice the loveliest thing each year should bear. You have owed long since the loveliness which Clytemnestra had borne to you, your daughter, Iphigenia. Summon your daughter now and keep your word.[17]

The Three Motifs in One Story

The above parallels only contain one or two of the three motifs which we have identified in the Jephthah story. The following two stories, that of Idomenus and of Maeander, contain all three of the Jephthah motifs.

According to Servius, the ancient commentator on Virgil, Idomenus, king of Crete, was caught in a storm on his return home from the Trojan war. He vowed to Poseidon, god of the sea, that if he were saved he would sacrifice to him the first thing that met him on his arrival home. On his safe return, the first thing that met him was his own son. According to some, Idomenus sacrificed his son; according to others, he only attempted to do so. In any event, a plague broke out over Crete, and the inhabitants, taking this to be a sign of divine displeasure, banished Idomenus from their shores.[18]

A similar tale is told by Pseudo Plutarch while explaining how a certain river in Asia got to be named Maeander. There was once an individual called Maeander, the son of Cercaphus and Anaxibia, who was at war in Phrygia with the people of Perssinus. During the war he vowed to the Mother of the gods that if she granted him victory he would sacrifice the first person who would come to congratulate him on his return home. It so happened that the first people who met him were his son, Archelaos, his mother, and his sister. In spite of their close relationship with him, he sacrificed them to satisfy his vow. But then, greatly grieved for what he had done, he cast himself into the river which from this time on was called by his name, Maeander.[19]

Implications for the Jephthah Story

Here are two stories closely paralleling the Jephthah story in all three of its principal motifs. Can the conclusion of these stories help elucidate the conclusion of the Jephthah story? Both stories would seem to support the sacrificialists' side in the Jephthah debate because Maeander actually sacrifices his family, and the plague unleashed upon Crete would lead one to believe that Idomenus did sacrifice his son, in spite of the difference of opinion recorded by Servius: "some say he sacrificed him, others he attempted to sacrifice him."[20]

On the other hand, the fact that Maeander commits suicide, and the fact of the plague and resulting expulsion of Idomenus, provides indirect support for the non-sacrificialists. For, had Jephthah really sacrificed his daughter, one would then, according to these parallels, have expected that something untoward would have happened either to Jephthah himself or to his land. But not a word is said in the story of the effect of the event upon Jephthah.[21] In support of this point, it may be recalled that after Mesha had sacrificed his firstborn son a plague also broke out, indicating the wrath of the deity (Chemosh or Yahweh?)[22] against the sacrifice.

Jephthah's Daughter and Iphigenia

The legend of Iphigenia is often mentioned, especially by sacrificialists, as an excellent parallel with the story of Jephthah's daughter.[23] But it should be pointed out that there are many forms of the Iphigenia legend, and none of them contains all three of the principal motifs of the Jephthah story. One, related by Euripides, as was seen above, contains the motif of making a rash vow resulting in the sacrifice of a beloved or only child. But the other motifs of the Jephthah story are absent. Indeed, in other versions of the legend a number of reasons are given as to why the goddess Artemis demands the sacrifice of Iphigenia. One reason is that the goddess was upset that Agamemnon had once boasted of being a better huntsman than Artemis herself, the goddess of the chase.[24] Another is that she was angry over an omen which Zeus had sent to guarantee Agamemnon's future success at Troy, in which two eagles, representing the Atridae, tore to pieces a pregnant hare in full view of the Greek army. Because Artemis was also protectress of wild animals, she became so angry at the suffering of the innocent creatures that she prevented the sailing of the ships and demanded the life of Iphigenia.[25] Still another version records that the goddess was punishing Agamemnon for a sin committed by his father, Atreus, who had broken a vow to sacrifice a golden lamb to her.[26] So while these versions contain a strong parallel of a father offering a daughter, they do not contain all the principal motifs of the Jephthah story. Furthermore, the fate of Iphigenia has been associated with two traditions. According to the tradition of Aeschylus, she was killed at Aulis:

> So then he [Agamemnon] hardened his heart to sacrifice his daughter that he might prosper a war waged to avenge a woman, and as an offering for the voyaging of a fleet! Her supplications, her cries of "Father", and her virgin life, the commanders in their eagerness for war reckoned as naught. Her father, after a prayer, bade his ministers lay hold of her as, enwrapped in her robes, she lay fallen forward, and with stout heart to raise her, as it were a kid, high above the altar.[27]

Likewise Cicero, in his *de Officiis*, in recording the version of the vow related by Euripides (his promise to sacrifice the most beautiful of a certain year), implies that she was sacrificed literally, inasmuch as he comments: "he ought to have broken his vow rather than commit so horrible a crime."[28] However, Euripides, in his *Iphigenia in Tauris*, following Hesiod's Cypria,[29] asserts that Artemis substituted a hind at the last moment and carried the maiden off to the land of the Taurians in the Crimea to be her priestess.[30] This tradition is also recorded by Apollodorus:

> So Clytaemnestra sent her, and Agamemnon set her beside the altar, and was about to slaughter her, when Artemis carried her off to the Taurians and appointed her to be her priestess, substituting a deer for her at the altar; but some say that Artemis made her immortal.[31]

Another play by Euripides, *Iphigenia in Aulis*, also has an ending in which Iphigenia is rescued, but most scholars believe that this ending is a later interpolation,[32] and that in the original play Iphigenia is actually put to death.

Summary

In sum, the parallels from outside literatures show a number of points in contact in various degrees with the Jephthah story. But, while these parallels are most interesting, they cannot be used by either side in the Jephthah debate with any degree of certainty. The fact that two of the stories, Idomenus and Iphigenia, record two traditions for their particular endings raises the intriguing question of whether there were two traditions associated with the ending of the Jephthah story as well. This, of course, would lend enormous support to my thesis concerning the intentional ambiguity of the present state of the Jephthah story.

Likelihood of Voluntary Celibacy and Consecration for a Woman in Ancient Israel

The third external consideration has to do with the likelihood that, from what is known elsewhere of Israelite society, a woman would elect through a vow or otherwise to remain celibate or consecrate herself to a sanctuary. The conclusion of celibacy for Jephthah's daughter was first proposed by the Kimḥi's in the 12th century,[33] and to it was added (particularly by Christian scholars) the idea that the daughter was consecrated to God for lifelong sanctuary service.[34] Both of these ideas are usually lumped together by proponents and opponents of the non-sacrificial theory, and an institution akin to that of the vestals or nunnery is envisioned.[35] For example, Bertheau, in a typical statement of opposition, declared: "there exists nothing in the Old Testament which mentions celibacy and cloisterlike withdrawal from the world in consequence of a vow."[36] Likewise, Zapletal observed: "If such an institution existed, it is remarkable that there is no mention of it in any legislation."[37] Similarly, Farrar stated: "If there had been any institution of vestals among the Jews we should without fail have heard of it, nor would the fate of Jephthah's daughter been here regarded and represented as exceptionally tragic."[38] But properly these two ideas should be separated, and the likelihood of a woman in Israel electing to remain celibate will be discussed first, and then the likelihood of a woman being consecrated for sanctuary service in ancient Israel.

Women's Electing to Remain Celibate

Opponents of the celibate conclusion point out emphatically that it is extremely unlikely for a woman in ancient Israel to have elected or vowed to remain celibate. There is no evidence whatsoever in the Bible for female asceticism.[39] On the contrary, in every period of Israel's history, marriage, not celibacy, is considered the desirable state for women.[40] The blessings of the married state are extolled, and it was held axiomatic that a woman achieved fulfillment only with husband and children.[41] Indeed, it was considered a tragedy for a woman not to be married, and a terrible misfortune, even a punishment, if she did not have children.[42] The institution of the levirate marriage is clear evidence of the importance for a wife to bear sons for her husband and was what Israelite society considered the norm: that a man's house and name should be continued in his children.[43] In such a society, it is thought that it would be highly unlikely for a woman to take a vow to voluntarily refrain from marriage and from having children.[44]

The non-sacrificialists do not disagree with this view of the primacy of marriage in Israelite society, but a few believe that it is possible to assume that some voluntary celibacy may have existed.[45] This assumption is based on the fact that, according to Numbers 6:2, women, as well as men, could vow themselves to God as Nazarites. Although the rules of the Nazarites, which specifically included abstinence from alcohol, not cutting the hair, and avoidance of corpses, did not include celibacy (the two most well-known Nazarites, Samuel and Samson, were both married), it is held most likely that this applied only to male Nazarites: they were permitted to marry, but a female one was not.[46] This is deduced from the fact that in ancient Israel a wife was considered the property of her husband.[47] A woman consecrated to God would, therefore, regard God as her spiritual husband, and would become, so to speak, His property. Hence, it would not be considered proper for such a woman to be married. She would remain in lifelong chastity or, in the case of a widow, in lifelong widowhood.[48]

Women's Electing to be Consecrated to Sanctuary Service

Once again the opponents of the celibate conclusion assert that there is no evidence in the Bible for women's serving at a sanctuary. In response, the proponents believe that the mention of the women doing something at the entrance of the Tent of Meeting in Exodus 38:8 and 1 Samuel 2:22 indicates that these women were performing some sort of sanctuary service.[49] The texts read:

> He [Bezalel] made the laver of copper and its stand of copper from the mirrors of the women who performed tasks (*ṣōb'ōt*) at the entrance of the Tent of Meeting . . . . [Exodus 38:8]

> Now Eli was very old. When he heard all that his sons were doing to all Israel, and how they lay with the women who performed tasks (*ṣōb'ōt*) at the entrance of the Tent of Meeting . . . . [1 Samuel 2:22]

The questions of who these women were and exactly what they were doing have never been satisfactorily answered.[50] Some of the non-sacrificialists believe that these women were those who had originally vowed to dedicate themselves to God, but did not avail of their option to redeem themselves through monetary redemption (Leviticus 27:1-8). Instead they elected to be assigned to the sanctuary.[51] There they would do non-ritual tasks "like cooking meals, making and mending garments, washing clothes, and keeping the general area clean."[52]

The term used for these women is *ṣōb'ôt*, and it has been noted that the verb *ṣābā'* "to serve," often having a military sense, is used figuratively to denote the militia sacra of the priests and levites in Numbers 4:23, 35, 39, etc. The leader and captain of the host is the God of Israel. By the side of this sacred militia it is claimed by some non-sacrificialists that there was this female band, the *ṣōb'ôt*.[53] However, others deny that the *ṣōb'ôt* were consecrated at all. These take the basic meaning of the verb *ṣābā'* as "to be in a multitude." The women of the passages are not ministering women but persons who collected together for the purpose of saying prayers, seeking requests, and offering thanksgiving.[54] This description is basically in accord with the traditional Jewish view of the *ṣōb'ôt* as pious women who came to the sanctuary to pray. Thus Onkelos renders *ṣōb'ôt* as "praying," LXX as "fasting." Ibn Ezra comments on the Exodus passage that

> these were pious women who presented their mirrors as an offering. They no longer had any need to beautify themselves, because they had renounced earthly desires. Instead they came daily to the entrance of the Tent of Meeting to pray and hear the words of the law.[55]

As far as the *ṣōb'ôt* are concerned, there is no indication given of the expected chastity or sexual status of these women.[56] Some scholars have conjectured that these women were in fact chaste,[57] others that they were the opposite, sacred prostitutes.[58]

Summary

There is no real evidence in the Hebrew Bible of women's electing to remain celibate, and the likelihood of this as a regular feature in society is remote. Likewise, there is little evidence in ancient Israel of an institution of celibate women being attached to a sanctuary akin to the chaste priestess in Mesopotamia (the *nadītu*,[59] *entu*,[60] *ugbabtu*[61]), or to the vestals in ancient Greece and Rome in the cults of Athene,[62] Artemis,[63] Vesta.[64]

A RARE EXAMPLE OF HUMAN SACRIFICE IN ISRAEL

Most Bible scholars today believe that the story of Jephthah and his daughter represents an example of a human sacrifice offered up in emergency conditions to obtain the active cooperation of the deity.[65] Another example of this type is the sacrifice, referred to earlier,[66] by Mesha, king of Moab, of his first-born son. Mesha, being invaded by the combined armies of Israel, Judah, and Edom, and seeing that the tide of battle was going against him, took his first-born son, and offered him up on the city wall as a burnt offering.

> So he took his first-born son, who was to succeed him as king, and offered him up on the wall as a burnt offering. A great wrath came upon Israel, so they withdrew from him and went back to [their own] land.[67]

The efficacy of the offering was immediate. The deed caused tremendous consternation upon the allies, and especially upon the Israelites. Thus, as with Mesha, it is believed that Jephthah was responding to an extraordinary situation, a desperate war with the Ammonites. Even if one grants that the war with the Ammonites be considered "emergency conditions" or a "specially dangerous situation,"[68] this view has, of course, to contend with an obvious and well-known problem. Given the fact that human sacrifice was abhorrent to Israel, a vow to make a human sacrifice would surely have been against the law. This being so, one would expect some condemnation of Jephthah in the text after he put his daughter to death.

Attempted solutions to this problem by sacrificialists have generally followed two lines: (1) it is held that a vow to offer human sacrifice was not in fact against the law in Jephthah's time, or (2) it is possible that Jephthah was unaware of the law.

Human Sacrifice Not Against the Law in Jephthah's Time

In advocating that a vow to offer human sacrifice was not against the law in Jephthah's time, a number of scholars point to the fact that the narrative does not seem to hold that such a vow is contrary to the spirit of Israelite religion.[69] Thus it is believed likely that in Jephthah's time human sacrifice could have taken place. Religious beliefs of this age must not be judged, say the sacrificialists, according to later laws or ideas; even the later prophets were forced to wage war against child sacrifice.[70] Soggin has recently pointed to the value of the Jephthah episode in enabling us to get a glimpse of early Israelite religion, telling us that it "had much more in common with that of Canaan and the other religions of the Ancient Near East than Israelites were able to record at a later stage or than the revisions of the text were disposed to admit."[71]

But there is an element here of *petitio principii.* It has first to be established that human sacrifice existed in ancient Israel before one can assume that the Jephthah episode is an example of it, and hence that it represents an earlier stage of Israelite religion. The fact is that it has never been satisfactorily established whether or not human sacrifice existed in Israel. The most recent studies on this old and difficult problem are those of Moshe Weinfeld[72] and Morton Smith,[73] who have debated the traditional view whether the reference to the passing of a child through fire or to Moloch indicates not child sacrifice but religious initiation to a foreign cult. The present state of inquiry seems to be that the evidence is such that one cannot say for certain one way or another whether human sacrifice existed in ancient Israel.[74]

Jephthah Unaware of the Law

The second attempted solution to explain Jephthah's action is that although a vow to offer human sacrifice was against the law, Jephthah was unaware of the law. In particular, he was unaware of those regulations in the Book of

Leviticus which would have made his vow invalid. This point of view is found in several *midrashim*.

In *Midrash Tanḥuma* Jephthah is termed one "who was not a scholar," "one who was deficient in learning," and "one who never studied Scripture." Had he been aware of the Torah legislation, he would never have put his daughter to death.[75] Likewise, his contemporaries did not know the law because "the Almighty had hidden it from them";[76] so they were not able to find a way out to release Jephthah from his vow. Ps. Philo records the midrash that the daughter of Jephthah went to the sages for help, but none could help her because God had closed the mouth of the sages.[77] The chief reason given for the ignorance of both Jephthah and the sages is that, according to the prescriptions of Leviticus 27:1-8, his vow was entirely invalid. According to these regulations, a human being vowed to God could be redeemed by a monetary payment.[78] Thus Jephthah, according to these traditions, was unaware of a legal means by which he could have saved his daughter.[79]

A reason often given, particularly by modern scholars, for Jephthah's ignorance of the law is the fact that he lived outside of Israel for some time.[80] Jephthah may have been, just as we know Israel was, influenced by the religion of the neighboring people. The Book of Judges testifies to the fact that the Israelites worshipped the Ammonite god Milkom prior to their liberation by Jephthah;[81] so it could well be that during Jephthah's stay in the land of Tob as a freebooter or mercenary chief, he too came under the influence of foreign religion.[82] A basic element in this argument is the belief that the Ammonites, like others of Israel's neighbors, regularly practiced human sacrifice in their cult.[83] Thus, it is thought, Jephthah believed that just as other gods required human sacrifice, so did Yahweh.[84]

The non-sacrificialists are able to refute this point of view in two ways. First, as the parallel case of David shows, the fact that one lives the life of a freebooter or mercenary outside of Israel does not necessarily mean that, upon one's return, one cannot still live in accordance with the law of Israel. Having lived outside of Israel does not by itself point to ignorance of Israel's law. Second, as with the case of Israel itself, there is no convincing evidence that human sacrifice was practiced as a regular part of the cult of any of Israel's neighbors,[85] so that any alleged influence of this practice on Jephthah is most speculative.

No Condemnation of Jephthah in the Text

The final question to be considered here, if, in fact, there is a case of human sacrifice, is why there is no word of disapproval or any moral evaluation in the text of Jephthah's act.[86] Jephthah is depicted in the entire chapter as a true follower of Yahweh (verse 9); he wages war on behalf of Yahweh, and calls upon Yahweh to judge between Israel and Ammon (verse 27); the spirit of Yahweh comes upon him (verse 29),[87] and he makes his vow to Yahweh (verse 30). He is extolled as one of Yahweh's saviors in the Book of Samuel (1 Samuel 12:11), alongside Gideon, Bedan (possibly Barak or Samson), and Samuel himself.[88]

Is it likely, then, say the non-sacrificialists, that Jephthah, a true Yahwist, would have presented an offering which was anathema to Yahweh, and that this fact would not be commented on by the narrator?[89]

The usual answer to this question is that absence of condemnation has little significance. Firstly, it may point to the fact that human sacrifice was in fact current in Jephthah's day.[90] Secondly, even if this is not the case, there are other heroes in the Bible whose errant behavior is not condemned.[91] But if, as is generally agreed, the stories of Jephthah fit into the redactional framework of the Deuteronomist, then one would expect unlawful acts to be somehow condemned, either overtly or obliquely,[92] in accord with the didactic outlook of the Deuteronomistic school. It will be recalled that the narrator castigated Gideon for a much lesser crime with the Ephod (Judges 8:27). Absence of condemnation is therefore significant in judging a character's action. Jephthah is not only *not* condemned but referred to by the same Deuteronomist as a "savior of Israel," which is hardly an appellation to be applied to one guilty of such a crime.

Jewish tradition, however, does condemn Jephthah. It is thought that he and the High Priest of the time, Phineas, could have effectively saved the daughter had they so desired. But Jephthah refused to accept Phineas' authority, and Phineas was too proud to act on his own initiative:

> But was not Phineas there to absolve him of his vow? Phineas, however, said: He needs me, and I should go to him! Moreover, I am a High Priest, the son of a High Priest; shall I then go to an ignoramus? While Jephthah said: I am the chief of Israel's leaders, should I go to Phineas![93]

Because of their personal dispute, the daughter died: "between the two of them the maiden perished";[94] to which situation the popular proverb was applied: "between the midwife and the woman giving birth the young woman's child is lost,"[95] or in another version: "between the shepherd and the wolf the kid was torn to pieces."[96] For their failure to act, both Jephthah and Phineas were punished. Jephthah died a horribly painful death, while Phineas was stripped of his ministry. Jephthah's punishment is deduced midrashically from a later verse:

> Jephthah died by his limbs dropping off. Wherever he went a limb would drop off from him, and it was buried there on the spot. Hence it is written: "then Jephthah, the Gileadite, died, and was buried in the cities of Gilead" [12:7]. It does not say, "in a city of Gilead", but, "in the cities of Gilead."[97]

The Rabbis, albeit in a midrashic fashion, continue the didactic approach of the Deuteronomist by attempting to find in a later text some evidence that Jephthah's actions were condemnable.

Summary

The proponents of the sacrificial point of view believe that Jephthah's act is to be considered an example, like that of Mesha and his son, of human sacrifice offered up in an emergency. To offset the objection that such a vow and execution would have been against the law, some proponents maintain that a vow to offer human sacrifice was not against the law, and if it was, Jephthah was unaware of it. A possible reason offered for Jephthah's ignorance of the law is that he had lived outside Israel and was subject to foreign influences. The absence of condemnation of Jephthah by the narrator is pointed to by non-sacrificialists as proof that the vow and its fulfillment were not contrary to the laws of Yahweh in Jephthah's time. The sacrificialists, on the other hand, point to the absence of condemnation as proof that human sacrifice was acceptable in Jephthah's time.

CONCLUSIONS

In this chapter a summary will be presented of the arguments, discussed in the previous chapters, which bear on the fate of Jephthah's daughter. They are listed, as far as is possible, according to their respective occurrences in the story. First the arguments of those who favor a literal sacrificial conclusion are listed, along with arguments by this school against the conclusion of celibacy or consecration. Next the arguments of those who prefer the latter conclusion are presented, along with their arguments against the literal sacrificial conclusion. An attempt will then be made to weigh all the arguments together. My conclusion is that while I personally favor a non-sacrificial fate for Jephthah's daughter, the evidence is so ambiguous that it must be admitted that both conclusions are possible. In positing that this situation was not accidental, it will be pointed out that the narrator is a brilliant stylist and craftsman who is most familiar with Hebrew rhetorical devices. Such a craftsman could be quite capable of devising a deliberately ambiguous ending. Other examples of suggested intentional ambiguities in the Hebrew Bible will be presented, and the suggestion will be made that perhaps the fate of Jephthah's daughter is not the chief element of the story at all, rather Jephthah's rash vow is. The story in effect is one which illustrates the consequences of a hasty vow; a fine irony for a man whose forte is seen to be eloquence of speech and mastery of words.

Summary of Arguments

For a Sacrificial Conclusion

(1) The text of the vow clearly states: "I will offer him up for an *'ôlāh*," and this was put into effect in the fulfillment.[1]

(2) The despair of the father, and the lamentation of the daughter, are inexplicable unless the daughter is going to die.[2]

(3) The fulfillment states: "he did unto her as he vowed" which was "to offer her up as an *'ôlāh*."[3]

(4) The annual commemoration of mourning the daughter would make little sense unless the daughter is actually put to death.[4]

(5) There are parallels in classical mythology to the various motifs in the Jephthah story which result in actual sacrifice of people.[5]

(6) Structural parallels with the Isaac story indicate a sacrificial conclusion for the Jephthah story.[6]

(7) There is no evidence in the Hebrew Bible that women could be vowed to celibacy, a concept alien in Israel.[7]

(8) A conclusion of celibacy cannot explain Jephthah's daughter's lamenting her virginity for two months. If she were indeed to remain celibate, she would have the rest of her life for such lamentation.[8]

For a Conclusion of Celibacy and Consecration

(1) The phrase in the vow *wehāyāh laYHWH* can only mean consecration, not offering of a sacrifice.[9]

(2) The emphasis in the text is on the daughter's virginity.[10]

(3) The text states that the fulfillment of the vow was that "she did not know a man."[11]

(4) It is the conclusion of voluntary celibacy, which was unique in Israel, that forms the basis for the annual celebration of the unmarried maidens.[12]

(5) There is some evidence in the Hebrew Bible, and parallels in other ancient cultures, of women consecrating themselves, or being consecrated to sanctuary service, and having to live a life of chastity in this service.[13]

(6) It is not stated in the text that Jephthah put his daughter to death.[14]

(7) If the daughter were going to die, she would lament not only her virginity but also her life, and would want to spend her last days with her father, not away from him.[15]

(8) There is no condemnation of Jephthah anywhere in the Hebrew Bible which implies that his vow and subsequent fulfillment must have been consistent with the laws of Israel; hence, it was not human sacrifice.[16]

(9) Structural parallels with the Isaac story indicate a non-sacrificial conclusion.[17]

(10) Parallels with the Mesha story and classical mythology lead one to expect that had Jephthah put his daughter to death something untoward would have subsequently happened to him.[18]

Weighing the Arguments

As has been observed in the discussions in the preceding chapters, not all the arguments listed above are of equal weight. The strongest ones, in my opinion, for the sacrificialists, are numbers 1, 3 and 8; for the non-sacrificialists, numbers 2, 3, 6, 8 and 10. Nearly all the arguments are answered by the opposing school, some more satisfactorily than others. Thus the non-sacrificialists answer the three arguments of the sacrificialists as follows: (1) The phrase "I will offer him up for an *'ôlāh*" is to be taken symbolically or figuratively.[19] (3) The fulfillment refers to something else in the vow other than the phrase "I will offer him up for an *'ôlāh*."[20] (8) While it is true that the daughter will have plenty of time later to lament her virginity, she will not be able to do so with her friends and on the hills—two other important details of her request. The "hills" are a place of seclusion, a place she cannot go to later; the "friends" are those from whom she will soon have to part company.[21]

On the other hand, the sacrificialists answer four of the five arguments of the non-sacrificialists as follows: (2) The emphasis in the text is on the daughter's virginity because she is to die a virgin, the sacrifice being all the greater because she has no children. The phrase "to bewail my virginity" has to be taken figuratively to mean "to bewail my young life."[22] (3) The phrase "she did not know a man" is not to be taken as the fulfillment of the vow, but must be taken circumstantially to indicate the status of the daughter at her death: she died a virgin.[23] (6) The reason it is not stated in the text that Jephthah put his daughter to death is that the writing is elliptical and not all the details need to be supplied.[24] (8) There is no condemnation of Jephthah either because what Jephthah did was not against the law at that time, or because not all heroes who commit illicit acts are condemned by biblical authors.[25] There is no counterargument to number 10.

The evaluation of the above arguments and counterarguments must of necessity be subjective. For example, whether to take phrases like "I will offer him up for an *'ôlāh*" or "to bewail my virginity" literally or figuratively is the prerogative of each scholar. However, it seems that, on balance, the case for the non-sacrificialists is stronger, particularly because some of the counterarguments of the sacrificialists are a little tepid. Thus, the sacrificialists' necessity to interpret "to bewail my virginity" figuratively, to explain the lack of mention of Jephthah's putting his daughter to death as part of the elliptical mode of writing, to dismiss the lack of condemnation as being of little import, in addition to not being able to respond to the point that had Jephthah sacrificed his daughter, the biblical and classical parallels would require that something untoward happen to him; all these, in my opinion, make the case for the non-sacrificialists more convincing than that of their opponents.

The Seven Problems

However, having indicated my personal preference, it must not be forgotten that a number of these arguments are based on the interpretation of a text which, as has been shown, contains many problems, both linguistically and exegetically. The seven principal arguments are as follows: (1) Whether the original intent of the vow was the sacrifice of a human being or an animal.[26] (2) The structure of the vow shows lack of congruence between the condition and the promise.[27] (3) The wording of the vow is anomalous, and leads one to believe that some textual dislocation has taken place.[28] (4) What the meaning is of the daughter's request to go to the hills for two months with her friends to bewail her virginity.[29] (5) Whether the phrase *wehî' lō' yāde'āh 'îš* "she did not know a man" is to be taken as circumstantial or consequential.[30] (6) Whether the phrase *watehî ḥōq beyisrā'el* means "it became a custom in Israel" or "she became an example in Israel."[31] (7) What the nature is of the annual festival: one of mourning or of celebration.[32]

Deliberate Ambiguities

It has been posited above[33] that these problems may not have been entirely accidental, but could possibly represent ambiguities consciously devised by the narrator. He chose his words so that they would be open to a number of interpretations.[34] As far as the fate of Jephthah's daughter is concerned, in spite of the fact that we have indicated our partiality for the non-sacrificial conclusion, the fact remains that the text, as it stands now, admits the possibility of either conclusion. Was this deliberate? With the conclusion left up in the air, the suspense of the entire story is heightened. In many respects this is akin to classical folklore, inasmuch as there language is often intentionally ambiguous,[35] and it has been observed above that some classical legends have different endings corresponding to different traditions.[36] It remains to be demonstrated that our narrator was capable of such deliberate writing, and that such ambiguities are to be found elsewhere in the Bible.

THE NARRATOR AS A CRAFTSMAN

That the narrator of our story was an accomplished storyteller has been noted before. Certain literary features have been pointed out by various scholars. These include the irony of the sharp transition from joy to sorrow,[37] and the elliptical mode of writing—in that not all the dialogue is provided,[38] nor, according to some, the details concerning the culmination of the vow.[39]

Lately, Trible has drawn attention to the significant structural devices and arrangements of the story,[40] which enhance our appreciation of the narrator's artistry.[41] For example, Trible has observed the repetition of certain key phrases in the story like *yāṣā' liqrā't* "to go out to greet" (verses 31 and 34), *pāṣāh peh* "to utter a vow" (verses 35 and 36), *'āsāh l* "to do to / for" (verses 36, 37, and 39), and has drawn attention to the fact that other words and phrases evoke certain other contexts. Thus Jephthah's daughter coming out to greet him with *tuppîm* and *meḥōlôt* "timbrels and dancing" (verse 34) reminds one of Miriam in Moses' time coming out with *tuppîm* and *meḥōlôt* (Exodus 15:20), and of the women in the time of Saul and David, who likewise came out to greet them with *meḥōlôt* and *tuppîm* (1 Samuel 18:6). Or the use of the word *yeḥîdāh* "only one" to describe the daughter (verse 34) calls to mind Isaac's being termed the *yāḥîd* in Genesis 22.[42]

In addition, I point to the narrator's use of the so-called *command / wish-action sequence*, *'ēlekāh* "let me go" (verse 37), *lēkî* "go!" (verse 38), *wattēlek* "then she went" (verse 38); *'ebkeh 'al betûlay* "let me bewail my virginity" (verse 37), *wattēbk 'al betûleyhā* "she bewailed her virginity" (verse 38); his use of word play between the roots *kr'* and *'kr* in *hakrē'a hikra'tinî* "you have indeed brought me low"[43] and *'okray* "my troublers" (verse 35); his use of classical Hebrew style employing the verb and its cognate accusative three times, *wayiddar Yiptāḥ neder* (verse 30), *weha'alîtīhû 'ôlāh* (verse 31), *nidrô 'ašer nādar* (verse 39), and the infinitive absolute with the finite verb, *nātôn tittēn* (verse 30), *hakrē'a hikra'tinî* (verse 35). Furthermore, one must admire his usage of the verb *šûb* "to return" in three different contexts within the space of a few verses. He uses it when Jephthah makes the offer of his vow conditional on his returning home safely from battle (*bešûbî bešālôm* "when I return safely," verse 31). He uses it next when he proclaims that he cannot revoke his vow (*lō' 'ûkal lāšûb* "I cannot revoke it," verse 35), and finally when the daughter returns to him after the two months respite (*wattāšāb 'el 'ābîhā* "then she returned to her father," verse 39).

The question that must now be asked is this: could such a stylist have been unaware of all the ambiguities, mentioned above, which are inherent in his finished text? Is it not probable that the narrator, superb craftsman that he was, deliberately devised them? Such a phenomenon is not unknown in the Hebrew Bible, as shall be demonstrated next.

DELIBERATE AMBIGUITIES ELSEWHERE IN THE BIBLE

In an article entitled "An Equivocal Reading of the Sale of Joseph," Edward L. Greenstein presents two good examples of the phenomenon.[44] In the first example, which constitutes the major burden of his article, Greenstein points out the narrative's ambiguity in Genesis 37 concerning the chain of events that led to Joseph's servitude in Egypt. These ambiguities touch upon questions like: how did the brothers intend to murder Joseph? is Joseph saved by Judah or by Reuben? is he taken to Egypt by Ishmaelites or Midianites? Greenstein comments that "such narrative style, in which inconsistent lines of action are interlaced through the text, may have been familiar and acceptable to an ancient or preliterate audience."[45] "The reader," explains Greenstein, "is manipulated to vacillate 'between two intelligibilities.' *This effect may have been precisely the redactor's intention*" [my italics].[46] The second example concerns the entwining and overlapping of the two stories in Numbers 16: one of the secular rebellion by Dathan and Abiram; and the other of the religious rebellion by Koraḥ and his followers. The two stories are entwined so intricately that "the reader is often confused about precisely who is involved in what."[47] It is even unclear as to who the earth swallowed up (in verses 31 and 32): the secular rebels or the religious ones?

Greenstein further noted that in both cases the ambiguities served to blur one thing while setting up something else in greater relief. Thus in the first story, "by blurring the human factors leading to the enslavement of Joseph, the narrative sharpens our image of the divine factor in bringing it about."[48] Hence Greenstein concludes:

> An equivocal reading of the sale of Joseph leads to the realization that, in the view of our narrative, it is not crucial to our understanding of the story whether the brothers sold Joseph to the Ishmaelites or the Midianites kidnapped him. It is important, rather, to perceive that the descent of Joseph to Egypt and his subsequent rise to power there reveal divine providence in history.[49]

Similarly in the second story, the ambiguities serve to blur the image of both groups of rebels but emphasize the image of Moses, who emerges triumphant.[50] Perhaps in the Jephthah narrative there is an example of the same circumstance: the ambiguities surrounding Jephthah's daughter serve to blur her fate, but throw something else in sharper relief. This, in my opinion, is Jephthah's rash vow. The daughter, then, would not be the chief focus of the story at all (it will be recalled that she is not even mentioned by name), rather Jephthah's rash vow is.

JEPHTHAH'S RASH VOW

In support of the assumption that Jephthah's rash vow is the chief focus of the story is the fact that later Jewish tradition also was more interested in this aspect of the story than in the fate of Jephthah's daughter. Jephthah's vow was considered as rash and ill-considered as the requests of Eliezer, servant of

Abraham in Genesis 24:14,[51] and the promises of Caleb and Saul in Judges 1:12 and 1 Samuel 17:25. Jephthah is classed with the fools who do not distinguish between various kinds of vows.[52]

Eliezer's request was believed to be ill-advised because it was thought that his request was phrased in such general terms that an undesirable girl (either a foreigner,[53] a slave,[54] a harlot,[55] or a handicapped one[56]) might fulfill the conditions. Caleb's and Saul's promises, too, were deemed to be injudicious, because it was thought that likewise an undesirable (either a foreigner,[57] an illegitimate person,[58] or a slave[59]) might win their respective daughters' hand. However, in all the above cases, despite the ill-considered words, God intervened and saw to it that only desirable people fulfilled the conditions: Rebekah in Eliezer's case; Othniel in Caleb's case; and David in Saul's case.

Jephthah's vow, too, is put in the same category as the others, except that in Jephthah's case God does not intervene with a fitting conclusion. The tradition was particularly upset over the possibility that a ritual infringement might occur.[60]

> Said the Holy One, blessed be He, to him: "Then had a camel, or a donkey, or a dog come out, would you have offered it up for an *'ôlah*?"[61]

Hence the angry deity punished him by having his daughter fulfill the promise of the vow: "What did the Lord do? He answered him unfittingly and prepared his daughter for him."[62]

This motif of a person making a rash oath is, of course, found elsewhere in the Book of Judges and in other books. In Judges 17:2, Michah's mother curses the one who stole her silver, unaware that the thief is her own son. In Judges 21:8, the tribes of Israel curse whoever will give a wife to a Benjaminite; when the Benjaminites are almost exterminated, they have to find a subterfuge to avoid the consequences of their rash oath. Examples elsewhere in the Bible are Genesis 31:32, where Jacob unwittingly passes a sentence of death on his beloved Rachel,[63] and 1 Samuel 14:24, where Saul curses the man "that eats any food before night falls," and almost causes the death of Jonathan.[64]

Finally, as was mentioned above in a different context,[65] Cicero used the vow of Agamemnon, which, according to him, led to the death of Iphigenia, as an example of a hasty vow which should not have been fulfilled: "He ought to have broken his vow rather than commit so horrible a crime."[66] This is similar to how Rabbinic tradition views the Jephthah story: the story illustrates the consequences of a rash vow. "Jephthah asked in an unfitting manner, and God answered him in an unfitting manner."[67] From the Rabbinic point of view, Jephthah's vow was an illegitimate one but one from which he could have been absolved. Nevertheless, Jephthah was guilty of uttering a rash vow. There is a fine irony here. Jephthah, who has earlier proved himself to be a man of careful words,[68] in his successful negotiations with the elders and with his shrewd diplomatic representation to the Ammonites,[69] misspeaks the wording of his own vow! Thereby he condemns his daughter to a fate the exact nature of which remains a conundrum to this day.

NOTES

Introduction

1. Wilbur Owen Sypherd, *Jephthah and his Daughter: A Study in Comparative Literature* (Newark: Univ. of Delaware, 1948).

2. *Ibid.*, 112. A few more works since 1948 are listed by Bathya Bayer in "Jephthah: In the Arts," *Encyclopaedia Judaica*, vol. 9 (Jerusalem: Keter, 1972), 1344-1345.

3. Sypherd, *Jephthah*, 1.

4. *Ibid.*, 117, 118, 120, 123, 166 (#121), 170 (#134), 188 (#241).

5. Possibly because a sacrificial death is considered "more poetical"; see the remarks of Paulus Cassel, *The Book of Judges* (New York: Scribner, Armstrong, 1875), 177, n. 2.

6. Sypherd, *Jephthah*, 117, 155 (#75), 163 (#108), 167 (#122), 168 (#126), 174 (#146), 175 (#152), 178 (#174), 182 (#205). One playwright, J. S. Rittershausen, citing the indefiniteness of the biblical ending, offered two conclusions: in the first the daughter is dedicated to a life of virginity; in the second she dies. However, in a revised edition of the play some years later, the author opted solely for the conclusion of dedicating the daughter to a life of virginity (Sypherd, *Jephthah*, 167).

7. A detailed list of works on the subject written in these centuries may be found in Laur. Reinke, "Ueber das Gelübde Jephtha's," *Beiträge zur Erklärung des Alten Testamentes*, vol. 1, pt. 3 (Münster: Coppenrath, 1851), 424-427.

8. Laur. Reinke, *Das Gelübde* (1851), and A. van Hoonacker, "Le Voeu de Jephté," *Le Muséon*, 11 (1892): 448-469, and *Ibid.*, 12 (1893): 59-80.

9. The most recent articles dealing with the subject are those of Phyllis Trible, "A Meditation in Mourning: The Sacrifice of the Daughter of Jephthah," *USQR*, 36 Supplementary (1981): 59-73; Naftali' H. Frostig-Adler, "La Storia di Iefte," *ASE* (1964-65): 9-30; Elías C. Dell'Oca, "El Voto de Jefté (Jue. 11, 30-39)," Revista Bíblica, 26 (1964): 167-171.

10. M. R. James, *The Biblical Antiquities of Philo* (London and New York: Macmillan, 1917), 194.

11. William Whiston, *The Works of Flavius Josephus* (Auburn and Buffalo: John E. Beardsley, 1857, 145 [= chapter vii, sec. 10].

12. *Bereshit Rabbah* 60:3; *Wayyiqra Rabbah* 37:4; *Qohelet Rabbah* 10:17; *Midrash Tanḥuma on Beḥuqqotay*, 35; *Yalqut Shimoni on the Prophets*, 68.

13. In some texts the final comment is indicated as a *tosefta*, a marginal note. In Sperber's critical edition it is part of the text; see Alexander Sperber, *The Former Prophets* (Leiden: E. J. Brill, 1959), 73.

14. The remainder of the text may be found on p. 62, n.15.

15. A complete list with pertinent citations may be found in Reinke, *Das Gelübde*, 433-445, and in Vincenz Zapletal, *Das Buch der Richter* (Münster in Westf.: Aschendorff, 1923), 186.

16. Allan Menzies, ed., *Origen's Commentary on John* (Grand Rapids, Michigan: Wm. B. Eerdmans, 1951), 377.

17. Philip Schaff, ed., *Saint Chrysostom* (Grand Rapids, Michigan: Wm. B. Eerdmans, 1956), 434.

18. Chayim David Chavel, *Ramban's Commentary on the Prophets and the Writings* (Jerusalem: Qirya Ne'emanah, 1964), 31-32 [in Hebrew].

19. See p. 17 *infra*.

20. Comment on verse 31.

21. *Ibid.*

22. Comment on verse 39, and also at end of verse 31.

23. Comment on verse 31.

24. Isaac Abravanel, *Commentary on the Former Prophets* (Jerusalem: Sefarim Torah Weda'at, 1956), 130 [in Hebrew].

25. See p. 43 *infra*.

26. Comment on verse 39.

27. Cassel, *Judges*, 176-177.
28. C. F. Keil and F. Delitzsch, *Joshua, Judges, Ruth* (Edinburgh: T. and T. Clark, 1865), 393.
29. August Köhler, *Lehrbuch der biblischen Geschichte*, vol. 2, pt. 1 (Erlangen: Andreas Deichert, 1884), 102.
30. Eduard König, *Geschichte des Reiches Gottes* (Braunschweig and Leipzig: Hellmuth Wollerman, 1908), 190.
31. A full list of scholars on both sides may be found in George Foot Moore, *A Critical and Exegetical Commentary on Judges* (New York: Charles Scribner's Sons, 1895), 304.
32. Ernst Bertheau, *Das Buch der Richter und Ruth* (Leipzig: Weidmann, 1845), 163, and 2nd ed. (1883), 196-198.
33. John Sutherland Black, *The Book of Judges* (London: C. J. Clay and Sons, 1892), 80.
34. D. Karl Budde, *Die Bücher Richter und Samuel* (Giessen: J. Ricker, 1890), 126.
35. F. Buhl, "Jephta," ed. Albert Hauck, *J. J. Herzog's Realencyklopädie für protestanische Theologie und Kirche*, vol. 8 (Leipzig: J. C. Hinrichs, 1896), 646.
36. Heinrich Ewald, *The History of Israel* (London: Longmans, Green, 1876), 395.
37. Ernest Renan, *History of the People of Israel*, vol. 1 (Boston: Roberts Bros., 1896), 277.
38. Gottlieb Ludwig Studer, *Das Buch der Richter* (Bern, Chur and Leipzig: J. F. J. Dalp, 1835), 295.
39. Julius Wellhausen, *Die Composition des Hexateuchs und der historischen Bücher des alten Testaments* (1889; reprint ed., Berlin: Walter de Gruyter, 1963), 224.
40. Ewald, *History*, 395.
41. Karl Budde, *Das Buch der Richter* (Tübingen and Leipzig, J. C. B. Mohr [Paul Siebeck], 1897), 88.
42. Immanuel Benzinger, *Hebräische Archäologie* (Leipzig: Georg Olms, 1927), 356.
43. Gustav Boström, *Proverbiastudien* (Lund: C. W. K. Gleerup, 1935), 115-120.
44. Moshe Weinfeld, *UF*, 4 (1972): 134, n. 10.
45. Leon Wood, *Distressing Days of the Judges* (Grand Rapids, Michigan: Zondervan, 1975), 287-295.
46. Bibliographical details of these and other commentaries, including those of Alfons Schulz (1926), E. C. Rust (1961), John Gray (1967), and Arthur E. Cundall (1968), may be found in the bibliography.
47. The translation revolves on whether the phrase *wehî' lō' yāde'āh 'îš* in verse 39 is taken as circumstantial (e.g., "she had not known a man") or as consequential (e.g., "she did not know a man"); see *infra*, pp. 33-34.
48. See the standard works in these areas.
49. For example, see Bertheau, *Richter* (1845); 164, (1883), 194; Buhl, *Jephta*, 645; Moore, *Judges*, 304; F. W. Farrar "Judges" in *Ellicott's Commentary on the Whole Bible* (1882; reprint ed., Grand Rapids, Michigan: Zondervan, 1981), 235; Wilbur Owen Sypherd, *Jephthah and His Daughter* (Newark: Univ. of Delaware, 1939), 10.
50. Martin Luther, *Die Deutsche Bible* (Weimar: Hermann Böhlaus Nachfolger, 1939), 131.
51. Apparently the late William F. Albright had a similar opinion. In his prolegomenon to the reprinting of C. F. Burney, *The Book of Judges* (New York: Ktav, 1970), 22, he stated: "No new light has been shed by recent discovery on the meaning of the sacrifice of Jephthah's daughter, whether she was condemned to perpetual virginity or was to be a human sacrifice. The arguments on both sides are perhaps equally weak."
52. The term *'ôlāh* is normally translated as "burnt offering." While I prefer rendering "whole offering" (with J. Milgrom, "Book of Leviticus," *Encyclopaedia Judaica*, vol. 11 [Jerusalem: Keter, 1971], 140), in order not to prejudice the case one way or another, I shall leave the term untranslated. See also on p. 25 *infra*.
53. Robert G. Boling, *Judges* (New York: Doubleday, 1975), 206.
54. *Ibid.*, 207.
55. The principal arguments of both sides are listed in chapter 5, pp. 50-51.
56. This has already been noticed before, cf., e.g., König, *Geschichte*, 191: "the text leaves in obscurity the manner in which the vow is fulfilled."

57. Because there is no practical way of distinguishing a narrator from any later editor or redactor, I shall use the term narrator throughout this study.

The Vow: Verse 31

1. E.g., Numbers 22:11 (*hayyôṣē'*), Genesis 15:4 (*'ăšer yēṣē'*).
2. Cf. Moore, *Judges*, 299-300; Zapletal, *Richter*, 182, 186.
3. As argued by Yehezkel Kaufmann, *The Book of Judges* (Jerusalem: Kiryat Sepher, 1968), 226 [in Hebrew].
4. Boling, *Judges*, caption to illustration 8c and p. 208.
5. Cf. Moore, *Judges*, 300.
6. Zapletal, *Richter*, 186.
7. *Ibid.*
8. So Reinke, *Das Gelübde*, 462; Zapletal, *Richter*, 186; Martin, *Judges*, 154.
9. E.g., E. W. Hengstenberg, *Dissertations on the Genuineness of the Pentateuch* (Edinburgh: John D. Lowe, 1847), 107; Reinke, *Das Gelübde*, 462; Keil and Delitzsch, *Judges*, 385, n. 2; Farrar, *Judges*, 233.
10. Augustus Pfeiffer, *Dubia Vexata Scripturae Sacrae* (Dresden: Martin Gabriel Huebner, 1679), 356.
11. Keil and Delitzsch, *Judges*, 385; Reinke, *Das Gelübde*, 462.
12. Hengstenberg, *Dissertations*, 107; Reinke, *Das Gelübde*, 462. It is also a literary convention that the conquering hero be greeted ceremoniously on his return from battle; see most recently, Yochanan Muffs, *JJS*, 33 (1982): 81, n. 1.
13. Exodus 15:20.
14. I Samuel 18:6.
15. Thus the fact that his daughter met him was not at all accidental, so Walter Baumgartner, *ARW*, 18 (1915): 248-249.
16. Studer, *Richter*, 292; Reinke, *Das Gelübde*, 461.
17. Keil and Delitzsch, *Judges*, 385; Zapletal, *Richter*, 186; Frostig-Adler, *ASE* (1964-65): 14.
18. *Bereshit Rabbah* 60:3; *Wayyiqra Rabbah* 37:4.
19. "The faithful dog which runs out to greet his master in German folktales is not a factor in the Orient," Baumgartner, *ARW*, 18 (1915):245.
20. *Bereshit Rabbah* 60:3; *Wayyiqra Rabbah* 37:4.
21. Most recently Eliya Shahor, *Biblical Curricula: The Book of Judges* (Tel-Aviv: Or-Am, 1979), 123 [in Hebrew].
22. Kaufmann, *Judges*, 226.
23. *Ibid.* Moore, *Judges*, 299, declares this argument to be "trivial to absurdity" [*sic*].
24. Shahor, *Judges*, 123-124.
25. Studer, *Richter*, 292.
26. Kaufmann, *Judges*, 226.
27. Servius III:121 and XI:264. George Thilo and Hermann Hagen, *Servii Grammatici Qui Feruntur In Vergilii Carmina Commentarii* (1881, 1884; reprint ed., Hildesheim: Georg Olms, 1961), I:365; II:510, and see *infra*, p. 41.
28. Baumgartner, *ARW*, 18 (1915):244-245.
29. William W. Goodwin, *Plutarch's Morals*, vol. 5 (Boston: Little, Brown, 1870), 488. See *infra*, p. 41. Cf. also the Arabic story of Al Mundaḥir, who likewise vows the first person, see *infra*, p. 40.
30. *Ad loc.*
31. Cf. Zapletal, *Richter*, 182; W. Nowack, *Richter, Ruth u. Bücher Samuelis* (Göttingen: Vanderhoeck and Ruprecht, 1902), 108.
32. Israel Mahalman, "Jephthah and Jephthah's Daughter" in Israel Bible Society, *Studies in the Book of Judges* (Jerusalem: Qiryat Sepher, 1966), 339 [in Hebrew]; Arthur E. Cundall, *Judges* (Chicago: Inter-Varsity Press, 1968), 147.
33. Kaufmann, *Judges*, 226. Cf. Arnold B. Ehrlich, *Randglossen zur hebräischen Bibel*, vol. 3 (1910; reprint ed., Hildesheim: Georg Olms, 1968), 120-121.

34. This view is accepted by some fundamentalist scholars who observe that Jephthah having made the vow of the one he truly loved thought that God would intervene and somehow change things (Hengstenberg, *Dissertations*, 108). From a folkloristic point of view, the possibility that Jephthah might under certain conditions have to sacrifice his daughter would be thought to be a great act of heroism on his part, Baumgartner, *ARW*, 18 (1915): 245-246.

35. Kaufmann, *Judges*, 226.

36. It certainly cannot be considered as a preposition "to him," see *infra*, p. 25 and note 62 of this chapter.

37. See commentary of David Kimḥi on Judges 11:29.

38. E.g., Exodus 21:15. Other examples in Eduard König, *Historisch—Comparative Syntax der hebräischen Sprache* (Leipzig: J. C. Hinrichs, 1897), #375f.

39. E.g., Wood, *Distressing Days*, 294.

40. Cf. Zapletal, *Richter*, 187.

41. Baumgartner, *ARW*, 18 (1915): 243-245.

42. E.g., Boling, *Judges*, 206.

43. *Ibid*, 208.

44. Cf. Kaufmann, *Judges*, 226.

45. According to Simon B Parker, the original structure of the vow included the deity being addressed in the vocative as in Hannah's vow and the Ugaritic vow, *UF*, 11 (1979): 694.

46. Cf.*Ibid*, 699.

47. Cf.*Ibid*, 696.

48. Zapletal, *Richter*, 182; Ehrlich, *Randglossen*, 121; Friedrich Nötscher, *Das Buch der Richter* (Würzburg: Echter, 1953), 50.

49. Parker, *UF*, 11: 697; Ehrlich, *Randglossen*, 120; Zapletal, *Richter*, 182.

50. Ehrlich, *Randglossen*, 120.

51. A perusal of the Hebrew manuscripts collected by Kennicott and de Rossi shows that there are four which read *le'ôlāh*, not *'ôlāh*, Benjamin Kennicott, *Vetus Testamentum Hebraicum cum variis Lectionibus*, vol. 1 (Oxford: Clarendon Press, 1776), 500; G. B. de Rossi, *Variae Lectiones Veteris Testamenti*, vol. 2 (Parma: Ex Regio Typographeo, 1785), 121. This may simply indicate an error in copying, or that indeed some scribes in the Middle Ages were aware of the difficulty in the text and corrected it. It is interesting that this lack of a preposition on *'ôlāh* served as a basis in the dispute between Rabbi Yochanan and Resh Lakish whether Jephthah was liable to pay monetary compensation or not, see *Bereshit Rabbah* 60:3; *Wayyiqra Rabbah* 37:4; *Yalqut Shimoni on the Prophets*, 68, and *infra*, p. 47, and Chapter 4, n. 78.

52. Boström, *Proverbiastudien*, 116.

53. This point was noticed already by Boström, *Ibid.* Cf. Deuteronomy 27:6; 1 Samuel 6:14, 15; 1 Kings 9:25.

54. Ehrlich, *Mikrâ Ki-Pheschutô*, vol. 2 (Berlin: M. Poppelauer, 1900), 339. The commonly accepted view that the sacrifice was offered to Chemosh has been reiterated most recently by Baruch Levine, *In the Presence of the Lord* (Leiden: E. J. Brill, 1974), 25, and by J. Alberto Soggin, *Judges* (Philadelphia: Westminster, 1981), 216.

55. Coincidentally, Chemosh was also the losing god in that portion of Gileadite territory which was the cause of Jephthah's war with the Ammonites (see Judges 11:24).

56. *Midrash Tanḥuma on Behuqqotay*, 50.

57. See below p. 57, n. 52.

58. The standard definitions of *'ôlāh* may be found in George Buchanan Gray, *Sacrifice in the Old Testament* (1924; reprint ed., New York: Ktav, 1971), and in Ronald de Vaux, *Studies in Old Testament Sacrifice* (Cardiff: University of Wales, 1964), 27.

59. E.g., Moore, *Judges*, 304; Zapletal, *Richter*, 185; Soggin, *Judges*, 215.

60. König, *Geschichte*, 190. See *infra*, p. 33.

61. Hengstenberg, *Dissertations*, 113; Van Hoonacker, *Le Muséon*, 12: 76.

62. As do some earlier commentators (Auberlen and Dereser cited by Reinke, *Das Gelübde*, 469-470, and Buhl, *Jephta*, 646).

63. As rightly observed by Reinke, *Das Gelübde*, 470, and Zapletal, *Richter*, 188.

64. Reinke suggests that the lack of the expected preposition *lamed* on *'ôlāh* in the phrase *weha'alîtīhû 'ôlāh* is an indication that it is to be understood as figurative, Reinke, *Das Gelübde*, 474.

65. Reinke, *Das Gelübde*, 502; Hengstenberg, *Dissertations*, 108. Van Hoonacker, *Le Muséon*, 12: 77-80, takes the figure to be a metonomy, but I agree with Zapletal (*Richter*, 190) that neither this passage nor the one in I Samuel is a very good example of metonomy.

66. Keil and Delitzsch, *Judges*, 395.

67. Hengstenberg, *Dissertations*, 108; Reinke, *Das Gelübde*, 502.

68. Van Hoonacker, *Le Muséon*, 12: 77; Martin Noth, *Numbers* (Philadelphia: Westminster, 1968), 68. Cf., also the use of *'āšām* in Isaiah 53:10.

69. Keil and Delitzsch, *Judges*, 393.

70. For an attempted explanation of this by the sacrificialists, see *infra*, pp. 39-40.

71. Evaristus Mader, *Die Menschenopfer der alten Hebräer und der benachbarten Völker* (Freiburg im Breisgau: Herder, 1909), 155; Dell'Oca, *Revista Bíblica*, 26: 168-169.

72. Cf. Zapletal, *Richter*, 189.

The Daughter's Involvement: Verses 34-38

1. Some scholars (e.g., G. A. Cooke, *The Book of Judges* [Cambridge: Cambridge Univ. Press, 1918], 79; Nowack, *Richter*, 109) believe that Jephthah's daughter was fully aware of her father's vow.

2. See above p. 15.

3. The Masorah Magnah lists this form as one of the five examples when the masculine *mimmennû* designates a feminine. The other examples are Leviticus 6:8; 27:9; I Kings 22:43; 2 Kings 4:39.

4. Kimḥi *ad* verse 34. See also Abravanel, *Commentary*, 130.

5. Ehrlich, *Randglossen*, 121; Zapletal, *Richter*, 184.

6. Zapletal, *Richter*, 183, notes that Codex Alexandrius, which reads *agapētē* "beloved," possibly reflects *yedîdāh* instead of *yeḥîdāh*.

7. Burney, *Judges*, 321.

8. Ibid.; Moore, *Judges*, 301.

9. E. Theodore Mullen, Jr., *CBQ*, 44 (1982): 199, n. 36.

10. Much weight has been placed on this detail in the story by the sacrificialists, for it is claimed that only the impending death of his daughter could justify Jephthah's grief and the daughter's subsequent lament; see, e.g., Buhl, *Jephta*, 646.

11. Reinke, *Das Gelübde*, 506-507; van Hoonacker, *Le Muséon*, 12: 75. In answer to at least one sacrificialist's question as to why Jephthah should mourn if his daughter were to be consecrated to God (so, Mader, *Menschenopfer*, 155), Cassel responded by indicating that even Roman fathers took it sorrowfully when their daughters became vestal virgins, notwithstanding the great honor of such a vocation (Cassel, *Judges*, 176-177).

12. Cundall, *Judges*, 148.

13. This point was already raised by Kimḥi in his discussion on whether or not to read the *qerê mimmennāh* "from her" in verse 34. He notes, but rejects, the interpretation that states that because the daughter was not married "He [Jephthah] did not have from her any [grand]son or [grand]daughter."

14. Hengstenberg, *Dissertations*, 115; Mahalman, *Jephthah*, 339.

15. Zapletal, *Richter*, 186; John L. McKenzie, *The World of the Judges* (New York: Prentice Hall, 1966), 147. But Jewish tradition believed that Jephthah was not bound by his vow because it was unlawful, *Bereshit Rabbah* 60:3; *Wayyiqra Rabbah* 37:4; *Qohelet Rabbah* 10:17; *Midrash Tanḥuma on Behuqqotay*, 38; *Yalqut Shimoni on the Prophets*, 68.

16. *Bereshit Rabbah* 60:3; Targum on verse 39.

17. I Samuel 14:24-45.

18. McKenzie, *World of the Judges*, 147. In folklore, when the victim is unnamed in a vow, the precise choice of the sacrifice is left to the deity, Baumgartner, *ARW*, 18:244.

19. Translation: Boling, *Judges*, 206.
20. Bertheau, *Richter* (1883), 197.
21. Cassel, *Judges*, 175; Keil and Delitzsch, *Judges*, 392. Cf. Köhler, *Geschichte*, 102.
22. The other occurrence is in verse 20 where *welō' he'emîn Siḥôn* "Sihon did not believe [Israel to pass through his territory]" is to be emended on the basis of the parallel passages in Numbers 21:23 (*welō' nātan*) and Numbers 20:21 (*wayemā'ēn*) to *wayemā'ēn* "he refused."
23. Zapletal, *Richter*, 185.
24. H. M. Orlinsky, *JBL*, 61 (1942):92-97.
25. Max L. Margolis, *ZAW*, 21 (1901):272.
26. Orlinsky, *JBL*, 61:96.
27. For other suggestions, see Burney, *Judges*, 323.
28. *Midrash Tanḥuma on Behuqqotay*, 43; *Yalqut Shimoni on the Prophets*, 67.
29. *Shemot Rabbah*, 15:4.
30. N. H. Tur-Sinai *apud* Mahalman, *Jephthah*, 344.
31. Mahalman, *Jephthah*, 340.
32. Sypherd, *Jephthah* (1939), 14. It will be observed later that many scholars compare Jephthah's daughter with Iphigenia who is often identified with Artemis (see below pp. 42-43). According to Epiphanius, Jephthah's daughter was worshipped as a goddess Koré-Persophoné by the people of Shechem and is thus elevated to the rank of a deity by the side of Artemis herself [Sypherd, *Jephthah* (1939), 14].
33. Keil and Delitzsch, *Judges*, 392-393.
34. Cassel, *Judges*, 176.
35. König, *Geschichte*, 191.
36. See commentaries of David Kimḥi, Ralbag (Levi ben Gershom), and Abravanel on verse 40. This suggestion is ridiculed by Zapletal, *Judges*, 194.
37. For example, the NEB translates *we'ebkeh 'al betûlay* "and mourn that I must die a virgin." Likewise, it translates "and she died a virgin" for *wehî' lō' yāde'āh 'îš* in verse 39.
38. Moore, *Judges*, 302; Boling, *Judges*, 209.
39. Nowack, *Richter*, 51; 110. Texts which elucidate this idea are Genesis 16:1-5; 30:23; 1 Samuel 1:10f.
40. Nötscher, *Richter*, 51; Burney, *Judges*, 323-334 (citing Sophocles, *Antigone*, 890). Other classical examples are given by Sypherd, *Jephthah* (1939), 14-15.
41. Cooke, *Judges*, 124. Cf. Gilbert Murray, *The Rise of Greek Epic* (New York: Oxford University Press, 1960), 131-133
42. König, *Geschichte*, 192; Boström, *Proverbiastudien*, 117.
43. Köhler, *Geschichte*, 102; Cassel, *Judges*, 175.
44. Taken as metonomy: virginity > time of virginity > maidenhood, so, for example, Bertheau, *Richter* (1883), 193.
45. Jewish Publication Society, *The Prophets: Neviim* (Philadelphia, 1978), 80.
46. As clearly illustrated in Leviticus 21:13 and Deuteronomy 22:14-17. See also Keil and Delitzsch, *Judges*, 387; Boström, *Proverbiastudien*, 117.
47. Hengstenberg, *Dissertations*, 120; Keil and Delitzsch, *Judges*, 392.
48. Cassel, *Judges*, 175.
49. Köhler, *Geschichte*, 102; Cassel, *Judges*, 176; Keil and Delitzsch, *Judges*, 392.
50. Cassel, *Judges*, 175; Keil and Delitzsch, *Judges*, 392.
51. Cassel, *Judges*, 175.
52. Boström, *Proverbiastudien*, 117-118. Boström also connects this phrase to the annual festival which he claims is based on a ceremony in which the maidens used to offer their virginity to the deity (p. 119), see *infra*, p. 36. For a recent appraisal of alleged sacred prostitution in the Bible (and in Canaanite religion in general), see Daniel Nussbaum, "The Priestly Explanation of Exile and Its Bearing upon the Portrayal of the Canaanites in the Bible," Master's thesis, University of Pennsylvania, 1974, 62-81.

THE FULFILLMENT AND THE AFTERMATH: VERSES 39-40

1. König, *Geschichte*, 190. See also p. 25 above.

2. E.g., Budde, *Richter* (1897), 88; Nowack, *Richter*, 110; Moore, *Judges*, 302-303, Burney, *Judges*, 324. A circumstantial clause represents a second event as occurring at the same time as that reported in the lead clause, Francis I. Andersen, *The Sentence in Biblical Hebrew* (The Hague: Mouton, 1974), 65. Normally the verb in the circumstantial clause is a participle, but when the context calls for a negative, then a perfect tense may be used as here (*welō' yāde'āh*), cf. S. R. Driver, *A Treatise On The Use Of The Tenses In Hebrew* (Oxford: Clarendon, 1881), #162.

3. Boling, *Judges*, 207.

4. James D. Martin, *The Book of Judges* (Cambridge, 1975), 144. We have already pointed out above (p. 31) that in early Greek myths the human victim is nearly always a virgin. Some have suggested that the statement of the daughter's virginity indicates her "ritually pure state" necessary for the sacrifice; see B. Dinour *apud* Mahalman, *Jephthah*, 348, and König, *Geschichte*, 191.

5. Marie-Joseph Lagrange, *Le Livre de Juges* (Paris: Libraire Victor Lecoffre, 1903), 207; Cooke, *Judges*, 124.

6. Keil and Delitzsch, *Judges*, 393. König asks, "What would be the point of the statement 'she had not known a man' if she was going to be sacrificed? Was this condition crucial for the sacrifice?" (*Geschichte*, 191). Furthermore, Cassel adds that it is surely not an event of very rare occurrence, for young women to die before they are married (*Judges*, 176).

7. König, *Syntax*, #362n. Cf. Driver, *Tenses*, #160 Obs. An identical syntax is to be found in Isaiah 1:2, *bānîm giddaltî werômamtî wehēm pāše'û bî*, "I have reared children and brought them up, but they have rebelled against me." Cf., also, 1 Kings 2:8; 19:3-4.

8. König, *Syntax*, #362n; Cassel, *Judges*, 176. Moore believes that such a translation would have required the Hebrew to read without the personal pronoun *hî'*, e.g., *welō' yāde'āh 'îš* (*Judges*, 303).

9. The presence of the *athnachta* under *nādar* lends a measure of masoretic support to this interpretation, for it indicates that the following clause *wehî lō' yāde'āh 'îš* does not go with the preceding one containing the *athnachta* but is an independent clause.

10. Jewish Publication Society, *The Prophets*, 80.

11. Cf. Genesis 47:26.

12. Cf. Exodus 30:21.

13. Lagrange, *Juges*, 207, n. 40; Burney, *Judges*, 324.

14. Cooke, *Judges*, 124; Zapletal, *Richter*, 185.

15. The Targum interpreted *ḥōq* as "a prohibition," rendering *gezērāh*, and elaborated on the Hebrew: "It was hence prohibited in Israel for anyone to offer up a son or daughter as a burnt offering as Jephthah, the Gileadite, had done. He did not consult Phineas, the priest. Had he done so, she could have been redeemed through monetary compensation."

16. Karl Brockelmann, *Lexicon Syriacum* (1928; reprint ed., Hildesheim: Georg Olms, 1966), 53b.

17. König adopted this translation (*und sie ward zu einer Norm*) in his *Syntax*, #323h.

18. Generally taken as mere variants, see the commentaries *ad loc.*

19. Moore, *Judges*, 303.

20. Boling, *Judges*, 207.

21. Flemming Friis Hvidberg, *Weeping and Laughter in the Old Testament* (Leiden: E. J. Brill, 1962), 104-105.

22. See above p. 31.

23. Zapletal, *Richter*, 186.

24. Wood, *Distressing Days*, 291.

25. Budde, *Richter* (1897), 88; Nowack, *Richter*, 110; Burney, *Judges*, 325.

26. Cassel, *Judges*, 176; König, *Geschichte*, 100, 102.

27. See their respective commentaries on verse 40.

28. Boström, *Proverbiastudien*, 119.

29. Cassel, *Judges*, 176, n. 2. Cf. van Hoonacker, *Le Muséon*, 12: 74-75.

30. de Vaux, *Studies*, 66. Similarly, Cooke, *Judges*, xxxix.

31. Hermann Gunkel, *Genesis* (Göttingen, 1910), 240; Tur Sinai *apud* Mahalman, *Jephthah*, 342; B. Mazar *apud* Mahalman, *Jephthah*, 349; Soggin, *Judges*, 217.

32. See the discussions in Burney, *Judges*, 332-334; and Soggin, *Judges*, 218.

33. Hvidberg, *Weeping and Laughter*, 103; Ignaz Goldziher, *Mythology Among the Hebrews* (New York: Cooper Square, 1967), 96-97.

34. Goldziher, *Mythology Among the Hebrews*, 96-97; Theodor H. Gaster, *Myth, Legend, and Custom in the Old Testament* (New York & Evanston: Harper and Row, 1969), 431-432; John Gray, *Joshua, Judges and Ruth* (New York: Nelson, 1967), 338-339.

35. Martin, *Judges*, 146; Soggin, *Judges*, 217; Hvidberg, *Weeping and Laughter*, 103. Both Soggin and Hvidberg describe the Jephthah story as the "historicization of a myth."

36. Martin, *Judges*, 146.

37. Hvidberg, *Weeping and Laughter*, 103.

38. Boström's analogy from the cult of the Byblian Aphrodite as cited by Lucian is very misleading. All women in that cult did not, as Boström alleges (*Proverbiastudien*, 119), have to offer themselves for one day at Aphrodite's service. Only those women who refused to have their heads shaved were required to offer themselves. And the market for them was limited to foreigners only. For the most recent translation, see Attridge and Oden, *The Syrian Goddess (De Dea Syria) Attributed to Lucian* (Missoula, Montana: Scholars Press, 1970), 13-15 (on section 6).

39. Boling, *Judges*, 210; McKenzie, *World of the Judges*, 148.

40. Cf., for example, Hvidberg's explanation (following Alfred Jeremias, *The Old Testament in the Light of the Ancient Near East* [New York: G. P. Putnam's Sons, 1911], 169) that "the reference to 'four days' might indicate that they mourned for the dead deity for th ee days, but that the deity on the fourth day was revived (and celebrated his accession to the throne and his wedding?)," *Weeping and Laughter*, 103. For the suggestion that these four days represent intercalary ones, see Y. Yadin *apud* Mahalman, *Jephthah*, 353.

External Considerations

1. Edmund Leach, *Genesis as Myth and Other Essays* (London: Jonathan Cape, 1969), 37-38.

2. *Ibid.*, 38. Note that an argument could be made that the demand of obedience (b) should come before (c).

3. In the absence of a name mentioned in the Hebrew text, a plethora of names has been suggested for the daughter in the various midrashic and artistic treatments of this story. For example, Achsa, Adulah, Aheba, Ana, Arpi, Axa, etc., have been suggested; for a full list, see Sypherd, *Jephthah* (1948), 10, n. 1.

4. Phyllis Trible, *USQR*, 36 (1981): 63.

5. Jephthah, like Gideon, is uncertain of God's help, E. Theodore Mullen, Jr., *CBQ*, 44: 199, and n. 35.

6. Cf. above p. 29.

7. Trible, *USQR*, 36: 64.

8. McKenzie, *World of the Judges*, 148.

9. Trible, *USQR*, 36: 65.

10. *Ibid.*, 66; McKenzie, *World of the Judges*, 148.

11. Burney, *Judges*, 324; Moore, *Judges*, 302; Frostig-Adler, *ASE*, 1964-65: 22.

12. Trible, *USQR*, 36: 66.

13. *Ibid.*, and Frostig-Adler, *ASE*, 1964-65: 22.

14. Stith Thompson, *Motif Index of Folk-Literature* (Indiana: Indiana University Press, 1958), J 1169.4 (vow to sacrifice first thing one meets), M 177.1.1 (vow to a deity for success in battle), S 222 (promise of a child for release from danger), S 240-241 (child unwittingly promised), S 241 (homecomer's vow), V 17.3 (sacrifice to get help in danger); Sypherd, *Jephthah* (1939), 6-9; Gaster, *Myth, Legend, and Custom*, 430-431. Baumgartner combines the three motifs we have identified into one, *ARW*, 18: 240.

15. Adr. de Sainte-Thècle, *Journal Asiatique*, 6 (1825): 159-160; also cited by Sypherd, *Jephthah* (1939), 7.

16. Charles James Lyall, *Translations of Ancient Arabian Poetry* (London: Williams and Norgate, 1885), xxviii.

17. Witter Bynner, "Iphigenia in Tauris," pp. 117-187, in *Euripides II*, ed. David Grene and Richmond Lattimore (Chicago and London: Univ. of Chicago Press, 1956).

18. Servius III:121 and XI:264, Thilo and Hagen, *Servii Grammatici*, I:365; II:510.

19. Goodwin, *Plutarch's Morals*, 488. Cf. Gaster, *Myth, Legend, and Custom*, 430. Because this particular river was noted for its winding course, the term Maeander became a metaphor for any winding or mazing pattern; cf. English "to meander" and "a meandering river."

20. Thilo and Hagen, *Servii Grammatici*, I:365; II:510; H. J. Rose, "Idomeneus," in *The Oxford Classical Dictionary*, ed. N. G. L. Hammond and H. H. Scullard (Oxford: Clarendon Press, 1970), 540; Mark P. O. Morford and Robert J. Lenardon, *Classical Mythology* (New York: David McKay, 1971), 305.

21. Baumgartner, *ARW*, 18: 246.

22. See above p. 24.

23. Ewald, *History*, 395, n. 1; Burney, *Judges*, 332; Sypherd, *Jephthah* (1939): 12; Frostig-Adler, *ASE*, 1964-65: 9, and others.

24. James George Frazer, *Apollodorus: The Library*, vol. 2 (New York: G. P. Putnam's Sons, 1921), 191; Hugh G. Evelyn-White, *Hesiod: Homeric Poems and Homerica* (Cambridge: Harvard University Press, 1943), 493.

25. Herbert Weir Smyth, *Aeschylus*, vol. 2 (London: William Heinemann, 1946), 19.

26. Frazer, *Apollodorus*, 192; Cf. Michael Grant and John Hazel, *Gods and Mortals in Classical Mythology* (Springfield, Mass.: G. and C. Merriam, 1973), 248-249.

27. Smyth, *Aeschylus*, 23.

28. Walter Miller, *Cicero de Officiis* (London: William Heinemann, 1913), 371.

29. Evelyn-White, *Hesiod*, 495; Grant and Hazel, *Gods and Mortals*, 248.

30. Arthur S. Way, *Euripides*, vol. 2 (London: William Heinemann, 1919), 287.

31. Frazer, *Apollodorus*, 191-193.

32. Charles R. Walker, "Iphigenia in Aulis," in *Euripides IV*, ed. David Grene and Richmond Lattimore (Chicago and London: University of Chicago Press, 1958), 214.

33. See above pp. 8, 17-18.

34. See above p. 9. Note that F. Buhl both in the article *Jephta*, 645, and in the revised English translation "Jephthah" in *The New Schaff-Herzog Encyclopedia of Religious Knowledge*, ed. Samuel Macauley Jackson, vol. 6 (1907; reprint ed., Grand Rapids, Michigan: Baker Book House, 1950), 118, incorrectly reversed the process, stating that Kimḥi proposed consecration to which Christian exegetes later added celibacy!

35. Cf. Reinke, *Das Gelübde*, 483.

36. Bertheau, *Richter* (1883), 196.

37. Zapletal, *Richter*, 194.

38. Farrar, *Judges*, 235. Similarly, Mader, *Die Menschenopfer*, 156.

39. Nötscher, *Richter*, 51. Cassel observed that "even among the Talmudists a female ascetic is a phenomenon unheard of" (*Judges*, 176, n. 2).

40. Zapletal, *Richter*, 191; Bertheau, *Richter* (1883), 196.

41. John H. Otwell, *And Sarah Laughed. The Status of Women in the Old Testament* (Philadelphia: Westminster, 1977), 49-55.

42. The motif of the barren woman is, of course, common among the matriarchs; cf. Gerhard von Rad, *Genesis* (Philadelphia: Westminster, 1972), 191. As for cases of not having children being considered a punishment, cf. the punishment of Michal, wife of David, in 2 Samuel 6:23.

43. Roland de Vaux, *Ancient Israel*. Vol. 1 (New York and Toronto: McGraw-Hill, 1965), 38.

44. Zapletal, *Richter*, 194.

45. There are some cases of enforced celibacy in marriages where the husband has stopped having marital relationships. Cf. cases of David and Michal in 2 Samuel 6:23, and David and his concubines (in 2 Samuel 20:3) who are confined to living in *'almenût ḥayyût* "living widowhood."

46. Hengstenberg, *Dissertations*, 116.

47. van Hoonacker, *Le Muséon*, 12: 74; Köhler, *Geschichte*, 108; David Marcus, *JANES*, 10 (1978): 59.

48. Reinke, *Das Gelübde*, 484; Köhler, *Geschichte*, 102.
49. Reinke, *Das Gelübde*, 481; Köhler, *Geschichte*, 102.
50. As can be seen from all the standard commentaries on the Books of Exodus and Samuel.
51. Hengstenberg, *Dissertations*, 111.
52. Wood, *Distressing Days*, 288; cf. Reinke, *Das Gelübde*, 484.
53. Hengstenberg, *Dissertations*, 110.
54. Reinke, *Das Gelübde*, 485; Cassel, *Judges*, 176, n. 2.
55. Commentary *ad* Exodus 38:8. We note the reference in Luke 2:37 to women praying and fasting at the Sanctuary; cf. Reinke, *Das Gelübde*, 485. It is unfortunate that the new Union of American Hebrew Congregations' *Torah* has picked up the old suggestion of Dhorme (*Recueil Édouard Dhorme* [Paris: Imprimerie Nationale, 1951], 678-680) that the task of these women is illumined by an inscription of Tepti-ahar of Susa (W. Gunther Plaut, ed., *The Torah: A Modern Commentary* [New York, 1981], 674-675). While this inscription does mention women acting as guards at a sanctuary (by being locked up in it for the night!), there is no indication whatsoever that the duties of these women involved praying. For the improved text readings since Dhorme, see Erica Reiner, *AfO*, 24 (1973): 95-96. Guarding the temple precincts in ancient Israel was one of the responsibilities of the Levites, not of women; see J. Milgrom, *Studies in Levitical Terminology, I. The Encroacher and the Levite. The Term 'Aboda* (Berkeley: University of California Press, 1970), 8-16.
56. Bertheau, *Richter* (1883), 196; Zapletal, *Richter*, 192. Keil and Delitzsch note that the absence of any distinct statement by no means warrants denying the fact (*Judges*, 395).
57. The fact that these women were virgins makes Eli's son's crime all the greater (Hengstenberg, *Dissertations*, 117; Reinke, *Das Gelübde*, 482-483. The assignment of a number of captured Midianite virgins to the priests and levites in Numbers 31:40-41, 47 is little proof that women in God's service had to be chaste. In the first place, these women were captives, not Israelite women being consecrated out of their own freewill. Secondly, this story cannot be considered as typical of the Israelite cult because it is late and full of ficticious elements (cf. Noth, *Numbers*, 229; John Sturdy, *Numbers* (Cambridge: Cambridge University Press, 1976), 214-216.
58. E. O. James, *Myth and Ritual in the Ancient Near East*, (New York: Frederick A. Praeger, 1958), 127; Raphael Patai, *Sex and Family in the Bible and the Middle East* (New York: Doubleday, 1959), 149.
59. Rivka Harris, "The Nadītu Woman," in *Studies Presented to A. Leo Oppenheim*, ed. R. D. Biggs and J. A. Brinkman (Chicago: University of Chicago Press, 1964), 106-135, esp. 108.
60. *CAD, E*, 173b.
61. *Ibid.*
62. Zapletal, *Richter*, 193
63. *Ibid.*
64. H. J. Rose, "Vesta, Vestals," in *The Oxford Classical Dictionary*, ed. N. G. L. Hammond and H. H. Scullard (Oxford: Clarendon Press, 1970), 1116.
65. E.g., Burney, *Judges*, 320; Soggin, *Judges*, 216. For the belief among non-Israelites that sacrifice could effectively influence the behaviour of a god, see Mader, *Die Menschenopfer*, 159.
66. See above pp. 24, 42.
67. 2 Kings 3:27.
68. Nowack*Richter*, 108.
69. Burney, *Judges*, 320; McKenzie, *World of the Judges*, 148.
70. Kaufmann, *Judges*, 229.
71. Soggin, *Judges*, 218.
72. *UF*, 4 (1972): 133-154; *UF*, 10 (1978): 411-413.
73. *JAOS*, 95 (1975): 477-479.
74. Weinfeld, *UF*, 10:411.
75. *Midrash Tanḥuma on Behuqqotay*, 47, 51. Also *Yalqut Shimoni on the Prophets*, 67.
76. *Midrash Tanḥuma on Behuqqotay*, 51.
77. James, *Biblical Antiquities*, 192.
78. According to *Bereshit Rabbah* 60:3 and *Yalqut Shimoni on the Prophets*, 68, Rabbi Yohanan declared that Jephthah was liable for the daughter's monetary consecration; according to *Wayyiqra Rabbah*: 37:4 it was Resh Lakish who said Jephthah was liable.

79. It is interesting that Wood interprets these regulations of Leviticus 27 to show that not only was Jephthah not ignorant of the law but also that he acted in direct accord with it. According to him, these regulations concerning redemption only applied to a man; for a woman a choice was available. She could either be redeemed by money, or could be devoted to Tabernacle service. Jephthah, in Wood's opinion, did not take the easy route of redeeming, which he might have done, but instead devoted his daughter for service (*Distressing Days*, 293-294). The theory that Jephthah put his daughter to death, not according to the rules of vows of legitimate sacrifices, but according to the rules of the *ḥerem* "devoted object" (Leviticus 27:28), was already known and rejected by the medieval Jewish commentator Naḥmanides (Chavel, *Ramban's Commentary*, 32), and thoroughly refuted by Hengstenberg, *Dissertations*, 105.

80. Frostig-Adler, *ASE*, 1964-65: 29-30. According to Otwell (*And Sarah Laughed*, 71), the entire story of Jephthah may be non-Israelite in origin.

81. Judges 10:6.

82. Mader, *Menschenopfer*, 157, 159; Farrar, *Judges*, 233.

83. Bertheau, *Richter* (1883), 198; Nowack, *Richter*, 108; Zapletal, *Richter*, 195; Frostig-Adler, *ASE*, 1964-65: 29.

84. Otwell, *And Sarah Laughed*, 69.

85. Keil and Delitzsch, *Judges*, 391; McKenzie, *World of the Judges*, 147.

86. Nowack, *Richter*, 108; McKenzie, *World of the Judges*, 147-148; Martin, *Judges*, 145. Frostig-Adler, however, points out that the fact that the story has an unhappy ending is an indirect expression of the disapproval of the narrator of Jephthah's action, *ASE*, 1964-65: 22-23.

87. Many scholars have noted that the Spirit of the Lord only extended to Jephthah's military endeavors, and not to his vow (cf. Zapletal, *Richter*, 195; Frostig-Adler, *ASE*, 1964-65: 19). The Spirit comes on others who also do improper acts (e.g., Gideon, Saul, David), so Farrar, *Judges*, 234. The Spirit's coming on Jephthah, it is held, is only an indication that Jephthah has become a leader approved by God to be a judge.

88. Cf. also Sirah 46:11; Hebrews 11:32-34.

89. Köhler, *Geschichte*, 101; Keil and Delitzsch, *Judges*, 393.

90. See above p. 46, and Mader, *Die Menschenopfer*, 157.

91. Mader, *Ibid.*, 158; Zapletal, *Richter*, 195; David Zakkai *apud* Mahalman, *Jephthah*, 351.

92. Obliquely, being something untoward happening which, though not spelled out, is considered a punishment for previous errors or breaches of the law. So, for example, Samson is not openly condemned for violating the covenant (see now, Edward L. Greenstein, *Prooftexts* 1 [1981], 250). Or, Jacob is not overtly condemned (by another narrator) for deceiving Esau, but condemnation of his action is to be seen in the progress of his life's struggle (see Nahum M. Sarna, *Understanding Genesis* [New York: Schocken, 1978], 183-184).

93. *Bereshit Rabbah* 60:3; Cf. *Wayyiqra Rabbah* 37:4; *Qohelet Rabbah* 10:17;*Midrash Tanḥuma on Behuqqotay*, 38; *Yalqut Shimoni on the Prophets*, 68.

94. In all the sources mentioned in the previous note.

95. *Bereshit Rabbah* 60:3; *Yalqut Shimoni on the Prophets*, 68.

96. Samuel Yerushalmi, *The Book of Judges* (Jerusalem: Mosad Yad Ezrah, 1973), 178 [in Hebrew].

97. *Bereshit Rabbah* 60:3, and similar wording in the other sources mentioned in n. 93.

CONCLUSIONS

1. Pp. 10, 25. The pages given here and in the following notes refer to pages in the preceding chapters.

2. P. 29.

3. Pp. 10, 33.

4. Pp. 35-36.

5. P. 41.

6. Pp. 39-40.

7. Pp. 43-44.

8. P. 30.
9. Pp. 10-11, 14.
10. Pp. 31, 33-34.
11. Pp. 11, 33-34.
12. Pp. 35-36.
13. Pp. 44-45.
14. Pp. 25, 40.
15. Pp. 30-31.
16. Pp. 47-48.
17. Pp. 39-40.
18. P. 42.
19. Pp. 25-26.
20. Pp. 33-34.
21. Pp. 30-31.
22. Pp. 31, 33-34.
23. P. 33.
24. Pp. 39-40.
25. P. 48.
26. Pp. 13-18.
27. Pp. 18-19.
28. Pp. 19-25.
29. Pp. 29-31.
30. Pp. 33-34.
31. P. 34.
32. Pp. 34-37.
33. Pp. 12, 18.
34. Cf. Mahalman, *Jephthah*, 338, 354.
35. Cf. Baumgarten, *ARW*, 18: 243.
36. P. 43 above.
37. Mahalman, *Jephthah*, 339; Frostig-Adler, *ASE*, 1964-65: 20-21; Trible, *USQR*, 36: 63.
38. Burney, *Judges*, 322; Frostig-Adler, *ASE*, 1964-65: 22.
39. Moore, *Judges*, 302; Cundall, *Judges*, 147; Mahalman, *Jephthah*, 340. Cf. Frostig-Adler's view that the act was so disgusting that the narrator does not record it (*ASE*, 1964-65: 22).
40. Trible, *USQR*, 36: 59-73.
41. Cf. Yehudah Shamir, *Hadoar* (May 30, 1980), 410, n. 14.
42. Trible, *USQR*, 36: 63.
43. Note that the suggested retroversion for Codex Vaticanus' *tarachē etarazas me* is *'ākôr 'akartanî*.
44. Kenneth R. R. Gros Louis and James S. Ackerman, eds., *Literary Interpretations of Biblical Narratives*, vol. 2 (Nashville: Abingdon, 1982), 114-125; 306-310.
45. *Ibid.*, 114.
46. *Ibid.*, 117.
47. *Ibid.*, 124.
48. *Ibid.*, 123.
49. *Ibid.*
50. *Ibid.*, 124. Another good example of a deliberate ambiguity has been shown by Menakhem Perry and Meir Sternberg in 2 Samuel 11 where the reader is unsure whether or not Uriah is aware of his wife's adultery, and whether or not King David thinks that Uriah knows anything, *HaSifrut*, I / 2 (1968): 263-292, and 449-452; *ibid.*, II / 3 (1970): 608-663, and 679-682.
51. The biblical text does not identify Abraham's servant, but Jewish tradition associates him with the Eliezer mentioned in Genesis 15.
52. *Qohelet Rabbah* 4:17 (18).
53. *Wayyiqra Rabbah* 37:4.
54. *Bereshit Rabbah* 60:3.

55. *Wayyiqra Rabbah* 37:4.

56. *BT Taanit* 4a.

57. *Wayyiqra Rabbah* 37:4.

58. *Ibid.*, and *BT Taanit* 4a.

59. *Ibid.* (*Wayyiqra Rabbah* and *Taanit*), and *Bereshit Rabbah* 60:3.

60. See p. 16 above.

61. *Bereshit Rabbah* 60:3; *Wayyiqra Rabbah* 37:4. Similarly, *BT Taanit* 4a.

62. *Bereshit Rabbah* 60:3; *Wayyiqra Rabbah* 37:4.

63. Jacob's vow in Genesis 28:20-22 is equated in *Bereshit Rabbah* 70:3 with Jephthah's vow. Both Jacob and Jephthah are termed people who "vowed and lost" as opposed to Israel (Numbers 21:2) and Hannah (1 Samuel 1:11) who "vowed and profited."

64. The admonition of being careful with one's speech is well known in wisdom literature, e.g., Job 5:2-5, cf. Tur-Sinai, *apud* Mahalman, *Jephthah*, 342.

65. P. 42 above.

66. Miller, *Cicero de Officiis*, 371.

67. *Bereshit Rabbah* 60:3.

68. Cf. Mahalman, *Jephthah*, 341.

69. According to Zakkai, his negotiations with the Ammonites represent the acme of diplomatic skill, *apud* Mahalman, *Jephthah*, 342.

ABBREVIATIONS

AfO, *Archiv für Orientforschung*
ARW, *Archiv für Religionswissenschaft*
ASE, *Annuario di Studi Ebraici*
BT, *Babylonian Talmud*
CAD, *Chicago Assyrian Dictionary*
CBQ, *Catholic Biblical Quarterly*
JANES, *Journal of the Ancient Near Eastern Society of Columbia University*
JAOS, *Journal of the American Oriental Society*
JBL, *Journal of Biblical Literature*
JJS, *Journal of Jewish Studies*
JSOT, *Journal for the Study of the Old Testament*
UF, *Ugarit Forschungen*
USQR, *Union Seminary Quarterly Review*
ZA, *Zeitschrift für Assyriologie*
ZAW, *Zeitschrift für die Alttestamentliche Wissenschaft*

BIBLIOGRAPHY

Abravanel, Isaac. *Commentary on the Former Prophets*. 1520. Reprint with additions. Jerusalem: Sefarim Torah Weda'at, 1965 [in Hebrew].

Albright, William F. Prolegomenon to reprint of *The Book of Judges*, by C. F. Burney. New York: Ktav, 1970.

Andersen, Francis I. *The Sentence in Biblical Hebrew*. The Hague: Mouton, 1974.

Attridge, Harold, W., and Robert A. Oden. *The Syrian Goddess (De Dea Syria) Attributed to Lucian*. Society of Biblical Literature. Text and Translations 9. Graeco-Roman Religious Series 1. Missoula, Montana: Scholars Press, 1976.

Baumgartner, Walter. "Jephtas Gelübde Jud. 11 30-40." *ARW*, 18 (1915): 240-249.

Bayer, Bathya. "Jephthah: In the Arts." Vol. 9, pp. 1344-1345, in *Encyclopaedia Judaica*. Jerusalem: Keter, 1972.

Benzinger, Immanuel. *Hebräische Archäologie*. 3rd ed. 1927. Reprint. Hildesheim: Georg Olms, 1974.

Bertheau, Ernest. *Das Buch der Richter und Ruth*. Vol. 6, Kurzgefasstes exegetisches Handbuch zum Alten Testament. Leipzig: Weidmann, 1845. 2nd ed. S. Hirzel, 1883.

Black, John Sutherland. *The Book of Judges*. The Smaller Cambridge Bible for Schools. London: C. J. Clay & Sons, 1892.

Boling, Robert G. *Judges*. Vol. 6A, The Anchor Bible. New York: Doubleday, 1975.

Boström, Gustav. *Proverbiastudien: Die Weisheit un Das Fremde Weib in Spr 1-9*. Lund: C. W. K. Gleerup, 1935.

Brockelmann, Karl. *Lexicon Syriacum*. 2nd ed. 1928. Reprint. Hildesheim: Georg Olms, 1966.

Budde, D. Karl. *Die Bücher Richter und Samuel*. Giessen: J. Ricker, 1890.

———. *Das Buch der Richter*. Vol. 7, Kurzer Hand-Commentar zum Alten Testament. Edited by D. Karl Marti. Tübingen and Leipzig: J. C. B. Mohr (Paul Siebeck), 1897.

Buhl, F. "Jephta." Vol. 8, pp. 641-646, in *J. J. Herzog's Realencyklopädie fur protestanische Theologie und Kirche*. Edited by Albert Hauck. 3rd ed. Leipzig: J. C. Hinrichs, 1896.

———. "Jephthah." Vol. 6, pp. 118-119, in *The New Schaff-Herzog Encyclopedia of Religious Knowledge*. Edited by Samuel Macauley Jackson. 1907. Reprint. Grand Rapids, Michigan: Baker Book House, 1950.

Burney, C. F. *The Book of Judges*. 1918. Reprint. New York: Ktav, 1970.

Bynner, Witter. "Iphigenia in Tauris." Pp. 117-187, in *Euripides II*. The Complete Greek Tragedies. Edited by David Grene and Richmond Lattimore. Chicago and London: University of Chicago Press, 1956.

Cassel, Paulus. *The Book of Judges*. Translated by P. H. Steenstra. New York: Scribner, Armstrong, 1875.

Chavel, Chayim David. *Ramban's Commentary on the Prophets and the Writings*. Jerusalem: Qirya Ne'emanah, 1964 [in Hebrew].

Cooke, G. A. *The Book of Judges*. Cambridge: Cambridge University Press, 1918.

Cundall, Arthur E. *Judges*. Tyndale Old Testament Commentaries. Chicago: Inter-Varsity Press, 1968.

Dell'Oca, Elías C. "El Voto de Jefté (Jue. 11, 30-39)." *Revista Bíblica*, 26(1964): 167-171.

Dhorme, Édouard. *Recueil Édouard Dhorme*. Paris: Imprimerie Nationale, 1951.

Dinour, B. *Apud* Israel Mahalman.

Driver, S. R. *A Treatise on the Use of the Tenses in Hebrew*. Oxford: Clarendon Press, 1881.

Ehrlich, Arnold B. *Mikrâ Ki-Pheschutô*. Vol. 2. Berlin: M. Poppelauer, 1900.

———. *Randglossen zur hebräischen Bibel*. Vol. 3. 1910. Reprint. Hildesheim: Georg Olms, 1968.

Eliṣur, Judah. *The Book of Judges*. Jerusalem: Mosad Harav Kook, 1976 [in Hebrew].

Evelyn-White, Hugh G. *Hesiod: The Homeric Hymns and Homerica*. Cambridge: Harvard University Press, 1943.

Ewald, Heinrich. *The History of Israel*. Vol. 2. 3rd ed. Translated and edited by Russell Martineau. London: Longmans, Green, 1876.

Farrar, F. W. "Judges." Vol. 2, *Ellicott's Commentary on the Whole Bible*. Edited by Charles John Ellicott. 1882. Reprint. Grand Rapids, Michigan: Zondervan, 1981.

Frazer, James George. *Appollodorus: The Library*. Vol. 2. The Loeb Classical Library. New York: G. P. Putnam's Sons, 1921.

Frostig-Adler, Naftali' H. "La Storia de Iefte." *ASE*, 1964-65: 9-30.

Gaster, Theodor H. *Myth, Legend, and Custom in the Old Testament*. New York and Evanston: Harper & Row, 1969.

Goldziher, Ignaz. *Mythology among the Hebrews*. Translated by Russell Martineau. New York: Cooper Square, 1967.

Goodwin, William W. Plutarch's Morals. Vol. 5. Boston: Little, Brown, 1870.

Grant, Michael, and John Hazel. *Gods and Mortals in Classical Mythology*. Springfield, Massachusetts: G. & C. Merriam, 1973.

Gray, George Buchanan. *Sacrifice in the Old Testament*. 1924. Reprint. New York: Ktav, 1971.

Gray, John. *Joshua, Judges and Ruth*. The Century Bible. New York: Nelson, 1967.

Greenstein, Edward L. "The Riddle of Samson." *Prooftexts*, 1(1981): 237-260.

———. "An Equivocal Reading of the Sale of Joseph." Vol. 2, pp. 114-125, 306-310, in *Literary Interpretations of Biblical Narratives*. Nashville: Abingdon, 1982.

Gunkel, Hermann. *Genesis*. Vol. 1, pt. 1, Göttingen Handkommentar zum Alten Testament. Göttingen: Vandenhoeck & Ruprecht, 1910.

Harris, Rivkah. "The *Nadītu*-Woman." Pp. 106-135, in *Studies Presented to A. Leo Oppenheim*. Edited by R. D. Biggs and J. A. Brinkman. Chicago: University of Chicago Press, 1964.

Hengstenberg, E. W. *Dissertations on the Genuineness of the Pentateuch*. Vol. 2. Translated by J. E. Ryland. Edinburgh: John D. Lowe, 1847.

Hoonacker, A. van. "Le Voeu de Jephté." *Le Muséon*, 11(1892): 448-469; 12(1893): 59-80.

Hvidberg, Flemming Friis. *Weeping and Laughter in the Old Testament*. Leiden: E. J. Brill, 1962.

James, E. O. *Myth and Ritual in the Ancient Near East*. New York: Frederick A. Praeger, 1958.

James, M. R. *The Biblical Antiquities of Philo*. London and New York: Macmillan, 1917.

Jeremias, Alfred. *The Old Testament in the Light of the Ancient East*. Vol. 2. Translated by C. L. Beaumont, edited by C. H. W. Johns. New York: G. P. Putnam's Sons, 1911.

Jewish Publication Society. *The Prophets: Nevi'im*. A New Translation of the Holy Scriptures according to the Masoretic Text. 2nd. sec. Philadelphia: Jewish Publication Society, 1978.

Kaufmann, Yehezkel. *The Book of Judges*. Jerusalem: Kiryat Sepher, 1968 [in Hebrew].

Keil, C. F., and F. Delitzsch. *Joshua, Judges, Ruth*. Vol. 4, Biblical Commentary on the Old Testament. Translated by James Martin. Edinburgh: T. & T. Clark, 1865.

Kennicott, Benjamin. *Vetus Testamentum Hebraicum cum variis Lectionibus*. Vol. 1. Oxford: Clarendon Press, 1776.

Köhler, August. *Lehrbuch der Biblischen Geschichte: Alten Testamentes*. Vol. 2, pt. 1. Erlangen: Andreas Deichert, 1884.

König, Eduard. *Historisch-Comparative Syntax der hebräischen Sprache*. Leipzig: J. C. Hinrichs, 1897.

———. *Geschichte des Reiches Gottes*. Vol. 2., pt. 1, Grundrisse der Theologie. Braunschweig and Leipzig: Hellmuth Wollerman, 1908.

Lagrange, Marie-Joseph. *Le Libre des Juges*. Études bibliques. Paris: Libraire Victor Lecoffre, 1903.

Leach, Edmund. *Genesis as Myth and Other Essays*. London: Jonathan Cape, 1969.

Levine, Baruch A. *In the Presence of the Lord*. Leiden: E. J. Brill, 1974.

Luther, Martin. *Die Deutsche Bible*. Vol. 9, pt. 1, D. Martin Luthers Werke. Weimar: Hermann Böhlaus Nachfolger, 1939.

Lyall, Charles James. *Translations of Ancient Arabian Poetry*. London: Williams & Norgate, 1885.

McKenzie, John L. *The World of the Judges*. New York: Prentice-Hall, 1966.

Mader, Evaristus. *Die Menschenopfer der alten Hebräer und der benachbarten Völker*. Biblische Studien. Edited by O. Bardenhewer. Freiburg im Breisgau: Herder, 1909.

Mahalman, Israel. "Jephthah and Jephthah's Daughter." Pp. 332-355, in Israel Bible Society, *Studies in the Book of Judges*. Reports of the Bible Study Group in David Ben Gurion's House. Jerusalem: Qiryat Sepher, 1966 [in Hebrew].

Marcus, David. "Civil Liberties under Israelite and Mesopotamian Kings." *JANES*, 10(1978): 53-60.

Margolis, Max L. "A Passage in Ecclesiasticus and Judg. 11, 37." *ZAW*, 21(1901): 271-272.

Martin, James D. *The Book of Judges*. Cambridge Bible Commentary on the New English Bible. Cambridge: Cambridge University Press, 1975.

Mazar, Benjamin. *Apud* Israel Mahalman.

Menzies, Allan, ed. *Origen's Commentary on John*. Vol. 10, The Ante-Nicene Fathers. Grand Rapids, Michigan: Wm. B. Eerdmans, 1951.

Milgrom, J. *Studies in Levitical Terminology, I. The Encroacher and the Levite. The Term 'Aboda*. University of California Publications, Near Eastern Studies. Berkeley: University of California Press, 1970.

———. "Book of Leviticus." Vol. 11, pp. 138-147, in *Encylopaedia Judaica*. Jerusalem: Keter, 1971.

Miller, Walter. *Cicero De Officiis*. The Loeb Classical Library. London: William Heinemann, 1913.

Moore, George Foot. *A Critical and Exegetical Commentary on Judges*. International Critical Commentary. 2nd ed. New York: Charles Scribner's Sons, 1895.

Morford, Mark P. O., and Robert J. Lenardon. *Classical Mythology*. New York: David McKay, 1971.

Muffs, Yochanan. "Abraham the Noble Warrior: Patriarchal Politics and Laws of War in Ancient Israel." *JJS*, 33(1982): 81-107.

Mullen, E. Theodore, Jr. "The 'Minor Judges': Some Literary and Historical Considerations." *CBQ*, 44(1982): 185-201.

Murray, Gilbert. *The Rise of the Greek Epic*. New York: Oxford University Press, 1960.

Noth, Martin. *Numbers: A Commentary*. The Old Testament Library. Translated by James D. Martin. Philadelphia: Westminster, 1968.

Nötscher, Friedrich. *Das Buch der Richter*. Die Heilige Schrift in deutscher Übersetzung. Echter-Bible. Das Alte Testament. Edited by Friedrich Nötscher. Würzburg: Echter, 1953.

Nowack, W. *Richter, Ruth u. Bücher Samuelis*. Vol. 4, pt. 1, Handkommentar zum Alten Testament. Edited by W. Nowack. Göttingen: Vandenhoeck & Ruprecht, 1902.

Nussbaum, Daniel. "The Priestly Explanation of Exile and Its Bearing upon the Portrayal of the Canaanites in the Bible." Master's thesis. University of Pennsylvania, 1974.

Orlinsky, Harry M. "Critical Notes on Gen. 39:14, 17, Jud. 11:37." *JBL*, 61(1942): 87-97.

Otwell, John H. *And Sarah Laughed: The Status of Women in the Old Testament*. Philadelphia: Westminster, 1977.

Parker, Simon B. "The Vow in Ugaritic and Israelite Narrative Literature." *UF*, 11(1979): 693-700.

Patai, Raphael. *Sex and Family in the Bible and the Middle East*. New York: Doubleday, 1959.

Perry, Menakhem, and Meir Sternberg. "The King Through Ironic Eyes: The Narrator's Devices in the Biblical Story of David and Bathsheba and Two Excurses on the Theory of the Narrative Text." *HaSifrut*, 1 / 2(1968): 263-292, 449-452 [in Hebrew].

———. "Caution, A Literary Text! Problems in the Poetics and the Interpretation of Biblical Narrative." *HaSifrut*, 1 / 3(1970): 608-663, 679-682 [in Hebrew].

Pfeiffer, Augustus. *Dubia Vexata Scripturae Sacrae*. Dresden: Martin Gabriel Huebner, 1679.

Plaut, W. Gunther, ed. *The Torah: A Modern Commentary*. New York: Union of American Hebrew Congregations, 1981.

Rad, Gerhard von. *Genesis*. Rev. ed. Translated by John H. Marks. Philadelphia: Westminster, 1972.

Reiner, Erica. "Inscription from a Royal Elamite Tomb." *AfO*, 24(1973): 84-102.

Reinke, Laur. "Ueber das Gelübde Jephta's, Richt. 11, 30-40." Vol. 1, pt. 3, pp. 419-526, in *Beiträge zur Erklärung des Alten Testamentes*. Münster: Coppenrath, 1851.

Renan, Ernest. *History of the People of Israel*. Vol. 1. Boston: Roberts Brothers, 1896.

Rose, H. J. "Idomeneus." P. 540, in *The Oxford Classical Dictionary*. Edited by N. G. L. Hammond and H. H. Scullard. Oxford: Clarendon Press, 1970.

———. "Vesta, Vestals." Pp. 1115-1116, in *The Oxford Classical Dictionary*. Edited by N. G. L. Hammond and H. H. Scullard. Oxford: Clarendon Press, 1970.

Rossi, G. B. de. *Variae Lectiones Veteris Testamenti*. Vol. 2. Parma: Ex Regio Typographeo, 1785.

Rust, E. C. *Judges, Ruth, I & II Samuel*. The Layman's Bible Commentaries. London: SCM Press, 1961.

Sainte-Thècle, Adr. de. "Du culte des esprits chez les Tonquinois, extrait du Traité des Sectes religieuses chez les Tonquinois et les Chinois." *Journal Asiatique*, 6(1825): 154-163.

Sarna, Nahum M. *Understanding Genesis*. New York: Schocken, 1978.

Schaff, Philip, ed. *Saint Chrysostom*. Vol. 9, A Select Library of the Nicene and Post-Nicene Fathers. Grand Rapids, Michigan: Wm. B. Eerdmans, 1956.

Schulz, Alfons. *Das Buch der Richter und Das Buch Ruth*. Vol. 2, pts. 4 & 5, Die Heilige Schrift des Alten Testamentes. Edited by Franz Feldmann and Heinr. Herkenne. Bonn: Peter Hanstein, 1926.

Shahor, Eliya. *Biblical Curricula: The Book of Judges*. Tel Aviv: Or-Am, 1979 [in Hebrew].

Shamir, Yehudah. "Jephthah the Judge." *Hadoar*, May 2, 1980: 375-376; May 30, 1980: 409-410 [in Hebrew].

Smith, Morton. "A Note on Burning Babies." *JAOS*, 95(1975): 477-479.

Smyth, Herbert Weir. *Aeschylus*. Vol. 2. Loeb Classical Library. London: William Heinemann, 1946.

Soggin, J. Alberto. *Judges*. The Old Testament Library. Translated by J. S. Bowden. Philadelphia: Westminster, 1981.

Sperber, Alexander. *The Former Prophets*. Vol. 1, The Bible in Aramaic. Leiden: E. J. Brill, 1959.

Studer, Gottlieb Ludwig. *Das Buch der Richter*. Bern, Chur and Leipzig: J. F. J. Dalp, 1835.

Sturdy, John. *Numbers*. The Cambridge Bible Commentary on the New English Bible. Cambridge: Cambridge University Press, 1976.

Sypherd, Wilbur Owen. *Jephthah and His Daughter: An Introduction to a Study of Historical, Legendary, Mythological and Cult Relations*. Reprinted from Delaware Notes, 12th series. Newark, Delaware: University of Delaware, 1939.

———. *Jephthah and His Daughter: A Study in Comparative Literature*. Newark, Delaware: University of Delaware, 1948.

Thilo, George, and Hermann Hagen. *Servii Grammatici qui feruntur in Vergilii Carmina Commentarii*.Vol. 1. 1881. Vol. 2. 1884. Reprint 2 vols. Hildesheim: Georg Olms, 1961.

Thompson, Stith. *Motif Index of Folk-Literature*. Bloomington, Indiana: Indiana University Press, 1958.

Trible, Phyllis. "A Meditation in Mourning: The Sacrifice of the Daughter of Jephthah." *USQR*, 36, Supplementary (1981): 59-73.

Tur-Sinai, N. H. *Apud* Israel Mahalman.

Vaux, Roland de. *Studies in Old Testament Sacrifice*. Cardiff: University of Wales, 1964.

———. *Ancient Israel*. New York and Toronto: McGraw-Hill, 1965.

Walker, Charles R. "Iphigenia in Aulis." Vol 4, pp. 209-307, in *Euripides IV*. The Complete Greek Tragedies. Edited by David Grene and Richmond Lattimore. Chicago and London: University of Chicago Press, 1958.

Way, Arthur S. *Euripides*. Vol. 2. Loeb Classical Library. London: William Heinemann, 1919.

Weinfeld, Moshe. "The Worship of Molech and of the Queen of Heaven and its Background." *UF*, 4(1972): 133-154.

———. "Burning Babies in Ancient Israel." *UF*, 10(1978): 411-413.

Wellhausen, Julius. *Die Composition des Hexateuchs und der historischen Bücher des alten Testaments*. 3rd ed. 1889. Reprint. Berlin: Walter de Gruyter, 1963.

Whiston, William. *The Works of Flavius Josephus*. Auburn and Buffalo: John E. Beardsley, 1857.

Wood, Leon. *Distressing Days of the Judges*. Grand Rapids, Michigan: Zondervan, 1975.

Yadin, Y. *Apud* Israel Mahalman.

Yerushalmi, Samuel. *The Book of Judges: Yalqut Me'am Lo'ez of Yaakov Culi*. Jerusalem: Mosad Yad Ezrah, 1973 [in Hebrew].

Zakkai, David. *Apud* Israel Mahalman.

Zapletal, Vincenz. *Das Buch der Richter*. Vol. 7, pt. 1, Exegitisches Handbuch zum alten Testament. Edited by Johannes Nikel. Münster in Westf.: Aschendorff, 1923.

INDEX

Index of Biblical Citations

Index of Modern Scholars Citations

Index of Rabbinic Sources